The Gospel Hoax

οὐ γὰρ ἐστιν κρυπτὸν ἐὰν μὴ ἵνα
φανερωθῇ, οὐδὲ ἐγένετ ἀπόκρυφον
ἀλλ᾽ ἵνα ἔλθῃ εἰς φανερόν.

*For nothing has been hidden except to be
uncovered, nor anything made secret but
to come into the open.*

Mark 4:22

The Gospel Hoax

Morton Smith's Invention of *Secret Mark*

Stephen C. Carlson

Baylor University Press
Waco, Texas

Book Design by Diane Smith
Cover Design by Pam Poll

The images that appear in this book are in the public domain or are
otherwise permitted by law. Figures 6 and 7 can only be used as they
appear in this book by permission of Baylor University Press.
The Figures are credited as follows:
Figure 1: Albert S. Osborn
Figure 2: Kenneth W. Clark
Figure 3: Morton Smith
Figure 4: Morton Smith
Figure 5: Morton Smith
Figure 6: Stephen C. Carlson
Figure 7: Stephen C. Carlson, Kenneth W. Clark, and Morton Smith

Library of Congress Cataloging-in-Publication Data

Carlson, Stephen C.
  The Gospel hoax : Morton Smith's invention of Secret Mark / Stephen
C. Carlson.
    p. cm.
  Includes bibliographical references (p.   ).
  ISBN 1-932792-48-1 (pbk. : alk. paper)
  1. Smith, Morton, 1915-   . 2. Secret Gospel according to Mark.
  I. Title.
BS2860.S42C37 2005
229'.8--dc22

                                        2005026081

Printed in the United States of America on acid-free paper

Dedication
To Aili, my wife and my love

Contents

Foreword

During his visit to the library of the Mar Saba monastery in 1958, did Morton Smith happen upon a reference to a previously unknown version of the Gospel of Mark in a previously unknown letter of the important early church figure, Clement of Alexandria, or did Smith himself create this text, thereby producing one of the most sensational scholarly hoaxes of modern times? In the decades since Smith first made the purported letter of Clement public, with its tantalizing and provocative excerpts of a putative secret version of the Gospel of Mark, there have been occasional and unresolved controversies about its genuineness, and, consequently, in scholarly circles there has been a widespread uncertainty about what to make of the text. On the other hand, understandably reluctant to think that a scholar of Smith's standing would have stooped to such a hoax, and irresistibly drawn by the whiff of esoteric Christian practices and suppressed versions of the Gospel of Mark, some scholars have adopted the text as a trustworthy source to use in historical reconstructions of early Christianity. For these scholars especially, the stakes involved in questions about the alleged letter of Clement and "secret Mark" are high. But for everyone concerned about making use of any bona fide source for the study of Christian origins, the questions about secret Mark have large consequences, and elicit eager interest.

Moreover, beyond scholarly circles secret Mark has found a strong popular interest as well. This is perhaps partly because ours is a time of enormous popular curiosity about early Christian diversity, great sympathy for allegedly suppressed versions of ancient Christianity, and a touching readiness among the general public to accept various claims that scholarly and ecclesiastical intrigues have combined to cover up some early Christian teachings, texts and practices. In this atmosphere, it seems to require surprisingly little to generate a very receptive popular attitude toward a text like secret Mark. But is secret Mark a suppressed and long-forgotten gospel text, or is it a phantom-text, conjured by a particularly clever hoaxer to play to certain types of wishful thinking?

Stephen Carlson's study of the purported letter of Clement is small in size but packs a powerful punch. Others have raised questions about the text, and several scholars have lodged astute observations that suggest that it is a fake. But Carlson presents by far the most thorough investigation to date. Indeed, it is difficult to think of anything that he has left unexamined. He judiciously weighs all the observations and arguments of previous scholars for and against the authenticity of the text, and this in itself would make his discussion a valuable contribution. But, in addition, Carlson deploys a further battery of original observations, among which his analysis of the properties of the handwriting of the text opens up a whole new line of discussion. Drawing upon the forensic science involved in forgery-detection, Carlson gives what seems to me convincing evidence that this purported letter of Clement was penned by someone trying to pass it off as an eighteenth-century manuscript.

Furthermore, combining impressively thorough investigation of all the relevant historical issues with his training as a lawyer, Carlson marshals a powerful case that the most likely person who perpetrated the hoax is the internationally celebrated scholar of ancient Judaism and Christianity, Morton Smith, who presented this letter of Clement as a discovery made while cataloguing books in the Mar Saba library. Carlson argues that Smith uniquely had the abilities, the opportunity, and the motives.

I suspect that for most scholars, Carlson's rather well-researched and powerful case that Smith created this letter of Clement will comprise the really worrying matter. The charge that Smith fabricated the letter of Clement and that the putative excerpts from a secret Mark are phoney is not just academic tittle-tattle; it is genuinely disturbing. Some scholars (myself included) have suspected that the letter may be a fake, or have allowed for this possibility, but have been very reluctant to think that a respected member of the scholarly guild (even such a colorful character as Smith was) would bend his considerable abilities to fabricating a text and put it forth as genuine. Scholarship depends, to a greater degree than we sometimes realize, on trust, scholars abiding by self-imposed rules of the game. And the game is not supposed to involve such trickery. Indeed, for some scholars, this reluctance to think that Smith would do such a thing appears to be the major reason for treating the Clementine letter as genuine. So, if Carlson is right (and, so far as I can tell, he has presented a rather compelling phalanx of argumentation), then the case of secret Mark raises uncomfortable questions about the integrity of our scholarly culture. On the other hand, Smith was an unusually clever and impressively well-prepared scholar, so maybe we need not fear many other hoaxes so well crafted!

However, for scholars particularly, the more substantial question by far is whether the Clementine letter is genuine or a fake. Can this text be used as a valuable second-century primary source for historical investigation of early Christianity and the transmission-history of the Gospel of Mark, or is the letter really only a modern curiosity, an artefact of learned sleight-of-hand, an especially clever practical joke played upon scholars in the field, and therefore worthless for the study of

Christian origins? Of course, any suggestion of fakery justifiably raises the question about who might have prepared such an impressively deceptive text, and Carlson rises to this demand. But I want to emphasize that for the study of early Christianity the key matter is whether the Clementine letter is genuine. My judgment is that Carlson's case against the authenticity of the text is persuasive, decisive, practically unanswerable. Certainly, anyone who now wishes to treat the Clementine letter as a valid second-century text will first have to try to refute Carlson's case in at least an equally detailed and thorough manner. Carlson has now made it impossible to give secret Mark the benefit of doubt, or to sit on the fence and avoid the issue.

Carlson offers the results of a meticulous and amazingly wide-ranging investigation of sources, a detailed and creative analysis involving wholly new matters not previously addressed (such as study of the handwriting of the Clementine letter), and fascinating proposals that Smith himself embedded the text and his references to it with clever clues that it is a hoax. Also, helpfully pointing out the distinctions between a forgery (usually done for financial gain) and a hoax (usually intended more to demonstrate the cleverness of the hoaxer), Carlson emphasizes that the purported letter of Clement should be judged a particularly clever and spectacularly successful instance of a scholarly hoax.

As the case for any scholarly claim, Carlson's study will now be subjected to the judgment of other scholars concerned with historical investigation of early Christianity. But to give his case an adequate assessment will require a commitment to thoroughness and clear thinking equivalent to what Carlson demonstrates. I think I can safely estimate where fair-minded scholarship will come down in the end, recognizing Carlson's diligent and cogent exposure of Smith's letter of Clement and its references to a secret Mark as an impressive fake. But if the text is more appropriately placed in the curio cabinet than on the shelf of primary texts of early Christianity, we can at least be grateful that the matter appears now rather clearly settled. It will be disappointing to some, and others will say "I told you so." But the more important matter is that we can now get on with the very real demands of engaging the remaining genuine early Christian sources. And, I suggest, we should also probably allow ourselves a belated congratulatory laugh, with Morton Smith, over this ingenious fabrication that drew so much interest and for so long defied our best efforts to satisfy ourselves whether it was real or a hoax.

Larry W. Hurtado

Preface

I first heard of the *Secret Gospel of Mark* as a teenager in the mid 1980s when I read an extract of it quoted in the *Holy Blood, Holy Grail* series—a sensationalistic exposition of the supposed bloodline of Jesus Christ and Mary Magdalene, which has just resurfaced in the public's imagination as the background for the fictional thriller, *The Da Vinci Code*. Even though I was not very familiar with the New Testament back then, the extract from *Secret Mark*, with its sentences beginning with "and straightaway," appeared to me exactly like I expected the author of the *Gospel of Mark* to have written. *Secret Mark* did not make much of an impression on me, however, and I missed the homoerotic intimation at the end of the passage. Perhaps I was a bit too young to notice it, but the authors of the *Holy Blood, Holy Grail* series did not call attention to it presumably because it would have contradicted their central premise. Rather, they focused on what Clement of Alexandria, the person who supposedly quoted *Secret Mark*, had to say about suppressing heretical gospels.

The first time I realized that *Secret Mark* could well be a modern fake was in 1995 when a very spirited discussion sprang up on a couple of academic mailing lists around the time Andrew H. Criddle's article in the *Journal of Early Christian*

Studies (*JECS*) was published. Several scholars I had already respected even expressed their suspicions that it was forged by its discoverer, the late Morton Smith, a professor of ancient history at Columbia. Then I read Criddle's article, and I concluded that he presented a compelling statistical analysis that whoever wrote the letter attributed to Clement of Alexandria had tried too hard to make it look like Clement. It was overkill. Thus, I began wondering: if *Secret Mark* was a fake of some sort, what kind of a fake would it be? Was it the eighteenth-century idle musings of a bored Greek Orthodox monk or a Dutch humanist? More sinister possibilities also occured to me: Was Morton Smith a victim of a malicious forgery, or did he himself have something to do with it? And, if so, why? These questions did not have easy answers, and I recall thinking that it would be a great puzzle for someone else to solve one day because I was about to finish law school and begin a career as a patent attorney. I had no real inkling, however, that eight years later I would make my own attempt to solve the puzzle. This book is the result.

Three very different things in 2003 impelled me to try solving the mysteries of *Secret Mark*: a forgery controversy over an artifact, a Supreme Court opinion, and a special issue in an academic journal. The controversial artifact was the James ossuary, a limestone bone-box bearing the inscription: "James son of Joseph, brother of Jesus." In the spring of 2003, the Israeli Antiquities Authority announced that it was a forgery, and, with my trust in technology, I wanted to know what went wrong with the initial geophysical examination. I reread the report, this time critically, and I was shocked to discover how incompetent it was. Michael Turton made a comment about it on the Crosstalk mailing list. Turton observed that obtaining control over the process of authentication is an important component of what he called a "forgery arc." That comment stuck with me and led me to revisit how the document containing *Secret Mark* was authenticated.

As part of my vocation, I follow the written opinions and decisions of the U.S. Supreme Court. One case was *Lawrence v. Texas*, which struck down as unconstitutional state laws criminalizing consensual, same-sex sodomy. In the opinion, Justice Anthony Kennedy presented an insightful, historical overview explaining how societal and legal attitudes toward homosexual activity have greatly changed over the years. This became important later.

The third trigger was a set of three articles devoted to *Secret Mark* in the Summer 2003 issue of the *Journal of Early Christian Studies*. These let me know that the controversy over *Secret Mark* was still just as heated as it was back in 1995 and no more settled. In fact, I was getting frustrated that, except for the publication of some new color photographs of it in 2000, there had been little movement on the question—a "stalemate in the academy," as Charles Hedrick titled the lead article.

I wondered if a fresh look from a different approach might be more successful in ending the stalemate, and I decided to apply my legal training to see if I could get anywhere. To do so, I had to research the law to recognize relevant facts to the *Secret Mark* case, sift through the facts to identify the evidence I could use, and organize the evidence into a coherent story. In this case, the "law" constitutes the methods used by literary critics in evaluating forgeries, and I found that Anthony Grafton's book, *Forgers and Critics*, was immensely helpful. Grafton explains that literary forgeries become easier to detect with the passage of time because assumptions about the past, which the forger took for granted, become obsolete and then obvious. Thinking back to *Lawrence v. Texas*, I considered whether Grafton's criterion could be evident in *Secret Mark*'s treatment of homosexuality. I looked into how homosexuality was viewed or "socially constructed" in antiquity and realized that whoever wrote *Secret Mark* misunderstood it. Masquerading as an ancient text, *Secret Mark* exuded the sexual *mores* of the 1950s. No wonder it caught so much more attention than any other new gospel discovery!

After reading *Author Unknown*, Don Foster's experience of unveiling the anonymous author of *Primary Colors*, I also learned that purely literary arguments are not as persuasive to the general public as material evidence such as handwriting samples and confessions. Even though the literary analysis convinced me that I was on the right track, I knew I needed stronger evidence. My inspiration for finding the stronger evidence came from two places. First, my friend Jack Poirier told me that he possessed samples of Smith's handwriting and knew where to find more. Second, in his discussion on *Secret Mark*, Bart Ehrman mentioned the story of Dionysius the Renegade, who forged a play to fool his rival and was clever enough to encode the work's real nature within the play itself. By this time I had read enough of Smith's writings to suspect that, if he did have something to do with it, his sense of humor was such that he could have salted *Secret Mark* with clues, revealing its true nature. Now that I knew what to look for and where to look for it, all I had to do was to find it.

Because this is my first book, there are many people I would like to thank. First, I would like to thank my parents, who sacrificed to make sure that I had a well-rounded liberal arts education that included the classics, even though my focus was on computers. I would also like to thank James A. Bigger for teaching me Latin and giving me a taste for Greek, and Dr. Helen Pope at St. Stephen's School in Rome for agreeing to teach me Greek even though I was the only student who signed up for the class. Mark Goodacre, my fellow soldier in the synoptic problem, whom I have come to regard as a close friend, also deserves my gratitude for always challenging me to publish my ideas (the good ones, that is) even though my doctorate is in a different field. My 2001 article on Clement of Alexandria would not have been written, much less submitted to *New Testament Studies* for publication, without his encouragement. Little did I realize my involvement with Clement would not be over.

As for the book itself, I owe my appreciation to many people who listened to my ideas or read my drafts and shared their assessments with me. These include Mark Goodacre, of course, Andrew Criddle, Jeffrey Gibson, Jack Poirier, Jeffrey Peterson, Mark Matson, Edward Hobbs, Carl Conrad, Ken Olson, Michael Turton, Shawn Kelley, David Landry, Gail Dawson, and Ulrich Schmid. Julie C. Edison, a professional forensic document examiner, gave me very helpful advice. Jeffrey Gibson, in particular, deserves to be singled out for overcoming my reticence and insisting that I talk with Larry Hurtado and Bart Ehrman about this. Both Larry and Bart were very supportive and gave me much useful feedback. Larry also introduced me to my editor, Carey Newman of Baylor University Press, who continues to amaze me with his passion for my book, his knowledge of the publishing business and the biblical studies field, his challenging me on the "framing metanarrative," and his lining up the kind of peer review this book required. All the anonymous reviewers made very helpful comments and the book is much stronger as a result. All remaining errors, of course, are solely mine.

I would also like to express my appreciation to my friends, coworkers, and family for their encouragement and their patience in letting me express what I am doing, even if it must have seemed a little obscure. These include Scott, Jackie, Mike, and April in our small group; my law partner, Keth Ditthavong, along with Linda, Margo, Sera, Ti, and Stephen at the office; and my parents, my brother Chris, and my in-laws, especially Heli and Sven. In particular, Heli helped a lot with the index.

Most of all, I would like to thank and dedicate this book to Aili, my wife, my love, and mother of my children. Without her support, encouragement, prayers, and faith, this book would never have been completed.

Introduction

Secret Mark first became known to modern scholarship in 1958 when a newly hired assistant professor at Columbia University by the name of Morton Smith visited the monastery of Mar Saba near Jerusalem and photographed its fragments.[1] Announced on the heels of many spectacular discoveries of ancient manuscripts in the Near East, such as the *Dead Sea Scrolls* and the Nag Hammadi gnostic corpus, *Secret Mark* promised to be just as sensational, featuring a passage from a previously unknown, secret edition of the Gospel of Mark.

If its disclosure was sensational, its contents were stunning. The secret passage, written in Mark's characteristic style, told the story of a youth who had been buried in a tomb. His sister came to Jesus and begged him to resurrect her brother. Yet, unlike—or even contradicting—the Lazarus account in John, the youth was still alive when Jesus reached him. Stun turned to scandal as the secret gospel went on to narrate that "the youth comes to him, wearing a linen cloth over his naked body. And he remained with him that night, for Jesus taught him the mystery of the kingdom of God" (*Clement* 447). But this was not the end of the mysteries surrounding *Secret Mark*.

Compounding the mystery were the peculiarities of its preservation. Unlike the finds at Qumran and Nag Hammadi, *Secret Mark* was not preserved in any ancient document. It was

1

found as a quotation in a letter, also previously unknown, ascribed to Clement of Alexandria that was copied into the end papers of an early modern book. The book was an edition of the genuine letters of Ignatius printed in 1646,[2] but the handwritten copy of Clement's supposed letter was written at least a hundred years *later* than that because its Greek handwriting resembles that of the eighteenth century (*Clement* 1). Physical tests of the Dead Sea Scrolls can confirm their antiquity, for example, but no physical test of *Secret Mark*'s manuscript can confirm that its text is older than the 1700s.

In fact, no physical test had ever been performed on the manuscript because it had not been secured for laboratory study before it was lost. After Smith photographed the text in 1958, he left the manuscript in the tower library of the isolated monastery and did not return. The next time it was seen by western scholars was eighteen years later, when it was transferred to the Greek Orthodox Patriarchate library in Jerusalem for further study.[3] While there, the manuscript was removed from the book, photographed in color, and then misplaced.[4] Its current whereabouts are unknown, but, if it still exists, it is presumably somewhere in the Patriarchate library. Thus, the only surviving physical traces of this momentous text are the two sets of photographs taken first in 1958 and then in 1976. There is only a slender hope that the manuscript might reappear.

If *Secret Mark* was controversial because of its mix of sex and religion, it did not take long to add politics to the fray. When Smith published his findings in 1973, some of the reviews of his work were unusually strident and personal.[5] Shawn Eyer has conveniently surveyed these reviews and discussed one of the reactions as follows:

> Only one reviewer, Fitzmeyer [*sic*], saw it worthwhile to point out that Morton Smith was bald. Whatever importance we may attach to the thickness of a scholar's hair, it seems that detached scholarly criticism fails when certain tenets of faith—even "enlightened" liberal faith—are called into question.[6]

The personalization of the debate soon went beyond observations of Smith's follicles and led to insinuations of his forgery. Delicately but unmistakably, Quentin Quesnell broached the issue of forgery in 1975, generating a heated exchange the following year.[7] Neither Quesnell nor Smith gave ground and the controversy continued. Some took Smith's side on the antiquity of *Secret Mark* and explored how the canonical Mark could have been a censored version of *Secret Mark*.[8] Others occasionally questioned the authenticity of *Secret Mark* only to have Smith tenaciously counterattack the weaknesses of their arguments.[9]

Little was settled by Smith's death in 1991. If anyone was waiting for a deathbed confession, it did not come.[10] Perhaps exhausted over the unproductive battle, biblical critics began coalescing into the position that *Secret Mark* postdates the canonical Mark and was written sometime after the first century, perhaps during second-century Alexandria.[11] Larry W. Hurtado epitomizes the academy's attitude over the text as follows:

> Furthermore, as a good many other scholars have concluded, it is inadvisable to rest too much on *Secret Mark*. The alleged letter of Clement that quotes it might be a forgery from more recent centuries. If the letter is genuine, the *Secret Mark* to which it refers may be at most an ancient but secondary edition of Mark produced in the second century by some group seeking to promote its own esoteric interests.[12]

But this settlement has less to do with where *Secret Mark* belongs and more to do with where *Secret Mark* does *not* belong: biblical critics are assigning *Secret Mark* to a time just late enough to be ignored.[13] Because of the uncertainty over its authenticity, some scholars out of prudence, refuse to make use of *Secret Mark*, even when it supports their results.[14] Not only that, an increasing number of scholars are putting themselves on the record as questioning not only *Secret Mark*'s authenticity but also Smith's role in it.[15] In what has been aptly dubbed a "stalemate in the academy," the lingering controversy continues to overshadow any serious investigation into the contents of *Secret Mark*.[16]

Just because *Secret Mark* is being largely ignored does not mean that it is going away. It is still being invoked, though with some hedging, as a convenient illustration for early gospel traditions found outside the New Testament. For example, one scholar recently wrote: "Revisions of Mark seem to have gone on well into the second century since Clement of Alexandria knows of three versions of the Gospel of Mark: the novice, spiritual, and Carpocratian versions."[17] In 1999 the first doctoral dissertation on *Secret Mark* was written, and its author, Scott G. Brown, has followed up in 2005 with a book arguing that *Secret Mark* was actually written by the same author as the canonical Mark.[18] Even in this "rethinking" of *Secret Mark*, Brown's treatment of the arguments for its authenticity has stayed largely within the same well-plowed field that has changed so few minds over the past thirty years.[19]

Resolving the uncertainty over *Secret Mark*'s status requires a new examination of the evidence.

1

The Revelation of *Secret Mark*

The fragments of *Secret Mark* that Smith photographed are found in a letter copied into the end papers of a seventeenth-century edition of the genuine epistles of Ignatius. The letter is ostensibly from an early church father, Clement of Alexandria (d. 215), and addressed to someone named Theodore (*Theod.* I.1).[1] The letter begins by congratulating Theodore for opposing a second-century libertine sect, the Carpocratians, and proceeds to denounce the Carpocratians in very strong terms (I.2–11). In particular, the letter reassures Theodore that the Carpocratians were lying about what was taught in a secret edition of the Gospel of Mark:

> Now of the things they keep saying about the divinely inspired Gospel according to Mark, some are altogether falsifications, and others, even if they do contain some true elements, nevertheless are not reported truly. For the true things being mixed with inventions, are falsified, so that, as the saying goes, even the salt loses its savor (συγκεκραμένα γὰρ τἀληθῆ τοῖς πλάσμασι παραχαράσσεται ὥστε · τοῦτο δὴ τὸ λεγόμενον · καὶ τὸ ἅλας μωρανθῆναι). (I.11–15)

The letter then explains the origin of this secret edition of Mark as follows:

As for Mark, then, during Peter's stay in Rome he wrote an account of the Lord's doings, not, however, declaring all of them, nor yet hinting at the secret ones, but selecting what he thought most useful for increasing the faith of those who were being instructed. But when Peter died a martyr, Mark came over to Alexandria, bringing both his own notes and those of Peter (κομίζων καὶ τα ταυτοῦ [sic] καὶ τὰ τοῦ Πέτρου ὑπομνήματα), from which he transferred to his former book the things suitable to whatever makes for progress toward knowledge. Nevertheless, he yet did not divulge the things not to be uttered, nor did he write down the hierophantic teaching of the Lord, but to the stories already written he added yet others and, moreover, brought in certain sayings of which he knew the interpretation would, as a mystagogue, lead the hearers into the innermost sanctuary of that truth hidden by seven veils. Thus, in sum, he prepared matters, neither grudgingly nor incautiously, in my opinion, and, dying, he left his composition to the church in Alexandria, where it even yet is most carefully guarded, being read only to those who are being initiated into the great mysteries. (I.15–II.2)

After detailing the origin of this *Secret Mark*, the writer then quotes a passage from the text to refute a question that Theodore apparently had about this Gospel (II.20–21). The quoted passage describes the story of the resuscitation of a young man reminiscent of the raising of Lazarus in John, yet with a different ending:

And they come into Bethany. And a certain woman whose brother had died was there. And, coming, she prostrated herself before Jesus and says to him, "Son of David, have mercy on me." But the disciples rebuked her. And Jesus, being angered, went off with her into the garden where the tomb was, and straightaway a great cry was heard from the tomb. And going near Jesus rolled away the stone from the door of the tomb. And straightaway, going in where the youth was, he stretched forth his hand and raised him, seiz-

ing his hand. But the youth, looking at him, loved him and
began to beseech him that he might be with him. And going
out of the tomb they came into the house of the youth, for
he was rich. And after six days Jesus told him what to do and
in the evening the youth comes to him, wearing a linen
cloth over his naked body. And he remained with him that
night (καὶ ἔμεινε σὺν αὐτῷ τὴν νύκτα ἐκείνην), for Jesus
taught him the mystery of the kingdom of God. And thence,
arising, he returned to the other side of the Jordan.
(II.23–III.11)

This passage is quoted presumably in full to persuade
Theodore that *Secret Mark* did not contain what must have
troubled him:

> After these words follows the text, "And James and John
> come to him," and all that section. But "naked man with
> naked man," and the other things about which you wrote,
> are not found. And after the words, "And he comes to
> Jericho," the secret Gospel adds only, "And the sister of the
> youth whom Jesus loved and his mother and Salome were
> there, and Jesus did not receive them." (III.11–16)

Unfortunately, just as the author begins to explain what
these curious passages could mean, *Theodore* ends midsentence
right before Clement's "true explanation" could be expounded:

> But the many other things about which you wrote both seem
> to be and are falsifications. Now the true explanation and
> that which accords with the true philosophy—. (III.17–18)

Smith's disclosure of the two-and-a-half page text is packed
with much new information about early Christianity, much
more than its small size would normally indicate. If genuine, the
document not merely conveys two new gospel fragments, but it
also supplies the only direct evidence of a letter from Clement,
a new *testimonium* on the origin of the Gospel of Mark, and the
earliest witness for Mark in Alexandria. The text also contains
additional material about an obscure, second-century gnostic

sect, the Carpocratians. Few scholars are afforded the opportunity to discover a text as important as what Smith photographed at Mar Saba in 1958.

For such a lifetime discovery, no one could have been better prepared for *Secret Mark* than Morton Smith. Smith, while studying in Jerusalem on a traveling fellowship, had already visited Mar Saba once before in January and February of 1942 (*Secret Gospel* 1).[2] During this stay at Mar Saba, Smith toured the monastery, heard stories of manuscripts hidden in nearby caves, and visited its two libraries (*Secret Gospel* 4–5). Afterwards, Smith continued his studies at the Hebrew University in Jerusalem and completed his dissertation on parallels between the Gospels and Rabbinic writings (*Secret Gospel* 7–8).[3]

After serving as an Episcopal priest,[4] Smith eventually started work on a second doctorate from 1948–1950 under Werner Jaeger at Harvard, where he became interested in Greek patristic manuscripts (*Secret Gospel* 8). In 1951, Smith obtained a teaching position at Brown University and pursued this interest. For example, Smith traveled to Greece in 1951–1952 in search of manuscripts of Isidore of Pelusium, where he inspected, photographed, and transcribed dozens of Greek manuscripts, many of which he dated to the eighteenth century.[5] According to one of his letters dated January 26, 1953, Smith had taken about 5,000 photographs during this expedition.[6] These were unsettling times for Smith, however; he was denied tenure at Brown in 1955 and was a visiting professor at Drew before securing a position at Columbia in 1957 where he would spend the rest of his career.[7]

Smith's publications before the summer of 1958 exhibited his erudition in a wide range of subjects relevant to *Secret Mark*. For example, in 1955 Smith published a detailed analysis of Vincent Taylor's commentary on the Gospel of Mark.[8] He had both an intimate knowledge of monastic libraries with their eighteenth-century Greek texts and a fine grasp of patristic letter transmission.[9] While at Drew, Smith also became interested in an early third-century heresiological text, the *Philosophumena* of Hippolytus, a text that includes a description of the Carpocratians.[10] Smith's interest in Clement of Alexandria became evident as early as March 1958 when he published an article in the *Bulletin of the John Rylands Library* that cited Clement of Alexandria four times.[11]

Meanwhile, Smith had begun planning to revisit Mar Saba, located in territory then controlled by Jordan, and Smith wrote to Gershom Scholem, a professor at the Hebrew University in Jerusalem for whom Smith earlier worked as a research assistant. Smith stated that he would "spend the whole summer in the Near East, including a week in both Jerusalem and Istanbul, and a month in both Jordan and northern Greece, hunting for collections of manuscripts in the monasteries of Chalcidice (excluding Athos)."[12] Though exact dates are generally difficult to discern from Smith's writings, Smith revealed that he "visited Jerusalem in the summer of 1958" and obtained permission from the Patriarch, His Beatitude Benedict, to stay in the monastery of Mar Saba for two weeks and catalog its manuscript materials (*Secret Gospel* 9; *Clement* ix).[13]

The population at Mar Saba had been steadily decreasing since its height and by 1958 the number of monks had dwindled to thirteen.[14] Despite the small staff at the monastery, one of the monks escorted Smith to the library in the old tower every morning and stayed with him there (*Secret Gospel* 10). In the library, Smith inspected the books and set aside those that contained manuscript material. After identifying three or four such manuscripts, he was permitted to take them to his cell and study them overnight, and the next morning the materials would be returned (11). Smith described the circumstances of his most famous find at Mar Saba as follows:

> Then, one afternoon near the end of my stay, I found myself in my cell, staring incredulously at a text written in a tiny scrawl I had not even tried to read in the tower when I picked out the book containing it. But now that I came to

puzzle it out, it began, "From the letters of the most holy
Clement, the author of the *Stromateis*. To Theodore," and it
went on to praise the recipient for having "shut up" the
Carpocratians. The *Stromateis*, I knew, was a work by
Clement of Alexandria, one of the earliest and most myste-
rious of the great fathers of the Church—early Christian
writers of outstanding importance. I was reasonably sure that
no letters of his had been preserved. So if this writing was
what it claimed to be, I had a hitherto unknown text by a
writer of major significance for early Church history. . . . I
hastened to photograph the text and photographed it three
times for good measure. Next came the question of identifying the book into the back of which it was written. The
front cover and the title page were lost (most of the books in
the tower library had lived hard lives), and there was nothing on the spine, but I could see that it was an edition of the
letters of St. Ignatius of Antioch (another early Church
father). The preface had been signed by the famous seventeenth-century Dutch scholar, Isaac Voss. Voss' work on
Ignatius had been published several times, I knew, but it
occurred to me that I could date the edition by photographing the first and last preserved page and comparing them
with complete volumes so I took those. (The edition turned
out to be that of 1646.) Then the bell rang for vespers, and I
went off, walking on air. (*Secret Gospel* 12–13)

Returning to Jerusalem, Smith developed the photographs,
transcribed the text, and shared some information about the
text with Gershom Scholem (*Secret Gospel* 13–14). Although
Smith had demonstrated proficiency from his other cataloging
efforts in dating Greek manuscripts to the eighteenth century
based on the style of handwriting,[15] he realized during his visit
to the Near East that this text was sufficiently controversial to
warrant obtaining other opinions from some of his colleagues
in Athens before returning to the United States (22–23). The
fruit of Smith's cataloging was translated into modern Greek
and published in a periodical of the Patriarchate of Jerusalem
in 1960.[16] According to Smith's catalog, he dated fourteen

other manuscripts at Mar Saba to the eighteenth century (nos. 6, 11, 20, 22, 23, 26, 31, 34, 37, 42, 47, 48, 61, and 67), but the dating of the manuscript containing *Theodore* and *Secret Mark*, no. 65, was the only one that included acknowledgments of assistance.

Smith announced his secret gospel to a group of scholars at the 1960 annual meeting of the Society of Biblical Literature,[17] and then eventually published his findings in two books in 1973, one for specialists, *Clement*, and the other for the general population, *Secret Gospel*.[18] The information pertinent for evaluating the provenance and authenticity of Smith's texts is dispersed among these two books and in the modern Greek translation of Smith's 1960 catalog. The catalog presents information about the manuscript collection Smith examined in 1958, *Secret Gospel* gives details on the circumstances of Smith's visits to Mar Saba, and *Clement* details Smith's case for the authenticity of the texts.

Both books, *Secret Gospel* and *Clement*, expound an interpretation of *Secret Mark* that took Smith years to develop—involving water baptism, union with Jesus, the work of the Spirit, magic, ascent into the heavens, and liberation from the Law. Smith summarized the interpretation as follows:

> Thus from the differences between Paul's baptism and that of the Baptist, and from the scattered indications in the canonical Gospels and the secret Gospel of Mark, we can put together a picture of Jesus' baptism, "the mystery of the kingdom of God." It was a water baptism administered by Jesus to chosen disciples, singly and by night. The costume, for the disciple, was a linen cloth worn over the naked body. This cloth was probably removed for the baptism proper, the immersion in water, which was now reduced to a preparatory purification. After that, by unknown ceremonies, the disciple was possessed by Jesus' spirit and so united with Jesus. One with him, he participated by hallucination in Jesus' ascent into the heavens, he entered the kingdom of God, and was thereby set free from the laws ordained for and in

the lower world. Freedom from the law may have resulted in completion of the spiritual union by physical union. This certainly occurred in many forms of gnostic Christianity; how early it began there is no telling. (*Secret Gospel* 113–14)

Most of the initial reviews of Smith's work seemed impressed by his case for the antiquity of *Secret Mark* but equally mystified as to this interpretation Smith built upon it. The assessments ranged from the more respectful, e.g., "Smith's confidence in the reliability of Mark II and this exegesis of it, is misplaced,"[19] to the more outraged, e.g., "Characteristically, his arguments are awash in speculation."[20]

The reception of Smith's texts then took a decidedly different turn when Quesnell asked "the unavoidable next question," whether *Secret Mark* is a literary fake.[21]

2

Uncovering Literary Fakes

The stalemate over *Secret Mark* goes back to the debate between Quesnell and Smith when Quesnell dismissed all of Smith's extensive, internal arguments for the authenticity of *Secret Mark* with a single wave of the methodological wand: "Physical examinations alone can make certain we are not dealing with a contemporary."[1] Quesnell pointed out that the absence of a thorough, physical examination of the sole manuscript of *Secret Mark* raises the possibility of a contemporary hoax because the same tools that Smith used to authenticate the text on internal grounds can be used by a hoaxer to fabricate the text.[2] Quesnell's caution over the authenticity of *Secret Mark*, however, was not based on specific positive evidence such as errors in the manuscript or its text that *Secret Mark* was a recent fake.[3]

Despite the passage of nearly thirty years since Quesnell first raised his objections to the manuscript's unavailability, and more than forty-five years since Smith visited Mar Saba, a physical examination of the *Secret Mark* manuscript has yet to be performed, and the removal and loss of its pages makes any such examination unlikely in the near future.[4] As a result, continuing to insist on a physical examination of the two-and-a-half page manuscript can at best only prolong the stalemate and at worst call into question the academy's competence to authenticate works known only from modern-era copies and photographs.[5]

There is a way out of Quesnell's predicament. Quesnell properly insisted that the need for a physical examination is most acute in order to guard against a contemporary deception, but *Secret Mark* is now at least forty-five years old. If *Secret Mark* is a modern-era fake, "created or modified with the intention to deceive,"[6] then *Secret Mark* should be as vulnerable to the passage of time as other false documents that purport to originate from a much earlier time. As Anthony Grafton in his survey of Western literary forgeries explained:

> If any law holds for all forgery, it is quite simply that any forger, however deft, imprints the pattern and texture of his own period's life, thought and language on the past he hopes to make seem real and vivid. But the very details he deploys, however deeply they impress his immediate public, will eventually make his trickery stand out in bold relief, when they are observed by later readers who will recognize the forger's period superimposed on the forgery's. Nothing becomes obsolete like a period vision of an older period.[7]

Successful fakes are tightly coupled to the time in which they were created because they were designed to deceive a contemporary. By necessity, the faker has to include details intended for a victim who lives much later than the time of the false document's supposed creation.[8] For example, to be successful, a fake first has to catch the intended victim's attention to be successful; otherwise, the fake will simply be ignored.[9] Yet, the issues that attract attention in the faker's day often have more to do with their contemporary context than with what people in antiquity thought was important. As times change, so do the issues, and a fake crafted to exploit a burning issue of its day will become old-fashioned in the hindsight of history.

Mistakes are inevitable, and historical fakes can rarely withstand sustained scrutiny, especially in the physical artifact that embodies the fake.[10] Thus, a forgery's success often depends on misdirection, by inducing the intended audience to forgo somehow a detailed examination of the manuscript and overlook its flaws. A common technique is to control the authenticating process, commonly by offering an overwhelming, but ultimately misleading, mass of supporting documentation detailing how well the fake fits into contemporary expectations of what an important, revolutionary find should look like. This approach not only captures the intended target's interest, but it also prevents close inspection of the fake's flaws. The sheer volume of the accompanying documentation makes the arduous task of independently verifying every aspect of the new discovery seem potentially futile, especially if the fake promises to meet a long felt scholarly need.[11]

The critics who are most vulnerable to being deceived are those who are contemporary with the production of the fake because they do not have the benefit of the passage of time that eventually exposes many falsifications. If the false document was skillfully crafted to pass current contemporary standards, detecting the deception can be very difficult on internal grounds because both the creator and the critics are in the same ideological moment and using the same tools. As a result, both a solid chain of custody or "provenance" and physical examination of the manuscript are vital in authenticating any contemporary discovery. When a new discovery appears financially valuable, critics are usually very good at insisting on rigorous testing and provenance, because many falsifications are forgeries in the strictest sense, i.e., perpetrated with the intent not merely to deceive but also to defraud, usually for money or fame.[12]

Not all falsifications, however, are intended to be monetarily fraudulent, and the lack of a recognizable pecuniary motive may induce critics to relax their insistence on expensive and rigorous physical testing. This is especially true for hoaxes, which are designed to deceive society's critics as an intellectual challenge or for personal reasons, usually out of the enjoyment from fooling the experts. Nevertheless, such hoaxes have a vulnerability that strict forgeries lack—their psychological payoff depends on their eventual disclosure.[13] Accordingly, to prevent a hoax from backfiring by becoming too successful in its deception, it is not uncommon for the hoaxer to plant deliberate mistakes or jokes as clues to the fake's true nature. For example, in a forgery designed to fool a rival, Dionysius the Renegade wrote a play in the name of Sophocles in which he embedded an acrostic reading about his rival, "Heraclides is ignorant of letters."[14]

The applicability of these principles can be illustrated in two different types of scholarly fakes that have occurred in the field of biblical studies.[15] The first example is a strict forgery of four fragments attributed to Irenaeus of Lyons, published in 1712 by a respected Tübingen professor.[16] This scholar was Christoph Matthäus Pfaff, who claimed to have discovered the fragments in a library in Turin, but the manuscripts containing the fragments could never be located (6–7). Even though Pfaff produced a massive 647-page commentary in 1715, they were disputed almost immediately by Scipio Maffei and lingered thereafter under a cloud of doubt (7–9). By the late nineteenth century, scholars voiced serious doubts over the fragments. For example, in 1884 Theodor Zahn concluded that one of the fragments could not have been from Irenaeus because it cited Hebrews as Pauline (2). It was not until 1900 that Adolf Harnack demonstrated that Pfaff was the one who forged all four fragments, in part by connecting the contents of the fragments with a controversy current in Pfaff's time between Pietism and Lutheranism (66–69).[17]

In retrospect, it is not surprising that the Pfaff forgeries would involve a patristic writer like Irenaeus, because Pfaff lived at a time of raging theological conflicts in which manuscripts of patristic writers were repeatedly being discovered and cited for one side or another. In fact, the book into which *Secret Mark* was copied is a typical product of that age: a 1646 Greek–Latin edition of the shorter, genuine recension of Ignatius's letters, based on a manuscript recently discovered in Florence and used in a Protestant-Catholic controversy over the apostolic succession of bishops.[18]

While Pfaff's apparent motive for his forgery was to bolster a theological position, Paul R. Coleman-Norton probably composed his fake as a practical joke.[19] In 1950, while in the library of a mosque in Morocco he visited during World War II, Coleman-Norton published an article claiming to have found and transcribed an otherwise unknown saying attributed to Jesus (439–40).[20] This saying, which Coleman-Norton called an "amusing *agraphon*," was embedded in a commentary on Matthew 24:51 ("there will be weeping and gnashing of teeth") that presented a dialog between Jesus and a disciple who asked what would happen to people without teeth (443). Jesus' punch-line response was: "O thou of little faith, trouble not thyself; if haply they will be lacking any, teeth will be provided" (443, n. 18). In fact, jokes permeate Coleman-Norman's article. For example, the Greek text about the fate of toothless people had gaps exactly where the letter *theta* is supposed to be, which he explained as follows: "for some external agency with an affinity for three-letter combinations starting with θ has left a *lacuna* in the shape of a hole sufficiently large to pierce this part of three lines" (443, italics original). Thus, both the Greek text and the toothless person have difficulty with the letter *theta*. Presumably, the dentures provided to gnash the person's teeth would also help to pronounce that letter's dental sound.

Coleman-Norton initially submitted the article for publication to the *Harvard Theological Review*, whose editor then was Arthur Darby Nock, the same person to whom Smith would later dedicate his scholarly book, *Clement of Alexandria*. (The other book, *Secret Gospel*, was dedicated to "the one who knows.") Nock contacted a former student of Coleman-Norton at the nearby Princeton Seminary for more information about him. That person was Bruce Metzger, who informed Nock that he had heard Coleman-Norton tell the same joke in class before the war. Nock therefore refused to publish the *agraphon* without at least a photograph of the manuscript. Coleman-Norton was unable to provide this minimum level of evidence with the excuse that neither he nor his colleague was able to secure or photograph the manuscript before it had supposedly been acquired by someone else, never to be seen again. As a result, Coleman-Norton had to resubmit his article to a number of other journals before finding one that would eventually publish it.[21]

Metzger could deduce almost immediately that the amusing *agraphon* was a hoax because he knew Coleman-Norton had possession of the *agraphon*'s contents (the denture joke) prior to his supposed discovery of it.[22] Without an ability to predict the future, discoverers do not normally possess the subject matter of their unexpected finds. Coleman-Norton's article also contained other warning signs of fakery. For example, although the eleven-page article covered a wide range of marginally relevant topics, half of which were presented in long footnotes, it contained very little information that could be used to corroborate circumstances of the discovery. Quesnell noted that this mass of irrelevant information was actually part of the deception because "it distracts the reader's attention from the lack of basic evidence by inundating him with information about everything else."[23] Needless to say, the distraction did not fool Nock, who followed up by checking into Coleman-Norton's background and insisted on examining at least a photograph of it before Nock would consider publishing it.

Nock's instincts for identifying fakes were among the best of his day, but the five decades since its publication has taken its toll on Coleman-Norton's joke such that its falsity is now obvious. It looks very much like what people in the late 1940s expected a discovery of an ancient manuscript to be. The spectacular manuscript discoveries during this time of Toura (1941), Nag Hammadi (1945), and Qumran (1947) had already generated much academic and popular interest in the romance of finding and studying unknown, ancient texts from Arab deserts. This interest turned into frustration, if not desperation, when it began to take decades for these texts to be published. Coleman-Norton's *agraphon* was too good to be true for its time—its find-story involving a visitor to a Moroccan mosque during World War II played into the largely unsatisfied demand for texts discovered in Mediterrean locales. The content of the amusing *agraphon* also was a product of its time; its punch-line parodied the then-popular fire-and-brimstone style of preaching. By the early twenty-first century, however, interest in and preaching about Hell had waned.[24] For all these reasons, Coleman-Norton's text looks more like an artifact of its bygone time of the late 1940s than a genuine product of antiquity.

Like Pfaff's falsification, *Secret Mark* was accompanied by a massive commentary in two books totaling about 600 pages, so massive that Smith later apologized for it as being "dreadfully complex."[25] Like Coleman-Norton's hoax, *Secret Mark* appeared as another ancient text emerging from the Arab desert in the mid-twentieth century. Although *Secret Mark* was spotted in a monastery rather than a mosque, even that detail firmly belongs to the mid-twentieth century. The plot of a popular evangelical thriller, *The Mystery of Mar Saba*, originally published in 1940 but frequently reprinted afterwards, revolved around the discovery of a revolutionary, ancient text in the monastery of Mar Saba that turned out to be a forgery.[26] And the similarities do not end there. Both *Secret Mark* and the fictional discovery reinterpret a resurrection in the Gospels in naturalistic terms. *Secret Mark* contains a story suggestive of the raising of Lazarus except that the young man was still alive in the tomb when Jesus arrived, while the novel's text contains a firsthand account by Nicodemus confessing that he had stolen the body of Jesus from the tomb.[27] In addition, the 1947 printing of the novel even includes a copy of the Greek text of the fictional forgery on one of the fly papers of the book.[28] The parallels between *The Mystery of Mar Saba* and *Secret Mark* have even led one scholar to conclude: "The fact that *Secret Mark* came from Mar Saba is either strong proof of the text's authenticity, in that nobody would have dared invent such a thing in the 1950s, or else it is a tribute to the unabashed *chutz-pah* of a forger."[29]

Further reasons to suspect a hoax had been noticed by Bart Ehrman, who pointed out that "until recently no one had bothered to consider the significance of this letter of Clement appearing right where it does, in the end pages of Voss's 1646 edition of Ignatius. If the letter is authentic, the placement is a brilliant irony."[30] Ehrman found especially ironic both the identity of the book—which purged the Ignatian corpus of forged letters—and the content of the last page facing opposite Theodore—which castigated "'impudent fellows' who have 'interpolated' passages into ancient texts, with 'all kinds of nonsense.'"[31] While it is possible, as Smith put it, that "truth is necessarily stranger than history" (*Secret Gospel* 148), if it turns out that *Secret Mark* is a fake, Ehrman's observation means that the faker must have had a good sense of humor.

These parallels between *Secret Mark* and known fakes may be grounds for suspicion but are not proof. Rather, as Smith him-self argued, "the supposition of forgery must be justified by demonstration either that the style or content of the work con-tains elements not likely to have come from the alleged author, or that some known historical circumstances would have fur-nished a likely occasion for the forgery" (*Clement* 89, n. 1). To show that *Secret Mark* is not merely misattributed but a modern fake, the bar must be raised to require both prongs of Smith's disjunction: the evidence should both exclude its purported origin and include a distinctly modern origin. An even stronger and, hence, more persuasive case is made if both prongs can be established for all three distinct components of *Secret Mark*—the manuscript that was copied into the back of an old book, the contents of the letter addressed to Theodore from Clement of Alexandria, and the contents of *Secret Mark* itself. Likewise, if mistakes in each of the three components of *Secret Mark* are also explained more satisfyingly as a modern imitation, tied to a specific person or time, then the case for the modernity of *Secret Mark* becomes overwhelming. Finally, if the features that betray the modernity of *Secret Mark* are not merely accidental but deliberately planted, *Secret Mark*'s status as a modern hoax would be established beyond reasonable doubt.

The Modernity of the Mar Saba Manuscript

Of all the aspects of *Secret Mark*, the authenticity of the actual manuscript that Smith photographed has been both the least supported and the least disputed. Quesnell noted that out of over 450 pages of material, Smith's scholarly treatment, *Clement*, devoted only a scant three pages of text and three cropped photographs to authenticating the manuscript.[1] The main reason for the lack of further investigation into the manuscript has been its unavailability for physical testing,[2] so reassessment of the authenticity of the physical manuscript is by necessity confined within the limits that Smith had prescribed: the photographs of the manuscript.[3] This reassessment is especially intimidating because Smith thanked ten of his colleagues for determining that the hand should be dated to "about 1750, plus or minus about fifty years" (*Clement* 1).[4] Clearly, the prospect for finding something that ten different experts in early modern Greek paleography missed is daunting.

Although Smith's support for his dating is broad, it is not deep. Ten cursory examinations are not worth as much as one detailed study, and the quality of their results depends on the circumstances in which they were performed. Smith obtained his colleague's opinions as follows:

> Opinions about the hand: Most of the experts were consulted orally, so I reported only the substance of their opinions. I customarily showed the photographs without saying anything about them, and simply asked the date of the hand. In subsequent conversation I asked about suspicious details and possible forgery. Replies on these points were consistently negative and did not seem worth itemizing.[5]

The expert opinions that Smith relied upon were informal and oral. Smith did not obtain, preserve, and disclose any of their reports in writing, so it is impossible to verify whether Smith correctly understood their opinions or whether their opinions were qualified in any way. There is also no information as to how long Smith's colleagues had studied the handwriting, and it makes a difference whether they spent thirty minutes with no prior notice or their examination lasted an entire week. In fact, it is even difficult to determine what kind of reproductions Smith showed his colleagues. In 1975, Smith stated that he showed them "photographs," but his 1960 catalog referred to lower-quality Photostats or photocopies (modern Greek φωτοτυπίας) of the manuscript.[6] There is also no evidence that the experts had actually compared the handwriting with other manuscripts produced at Mar Saba. In fact, the only comparison sample published by Smith was that of Callinicus III, the Patriarch of Constantinople. This person, however, hailed from Thessaly; he was not a monk from Mar Saba in the Patriarchy of Jerusalem.

The open-ended nature of the consultation "without saying anything about them" did not put Smith's colleagues on notice about the possibility of imitation. It is hard to find evidence of forgery if one is not looking for it. Although Smith stated that he followed up about "suspicious details and possible forgery" in "subsequent conversation,"[7] Smith has provided no information as to what specifically those suspicious details were, which persons he asked, and whether they still had access to the photographs or had to rely on memory in reevaluating the details. In fact, Smith's odd use of the singular may only indi-cate a single "conversation."

In short, Smith's reporting of those consultations did little more than state that the manuscript generally looks like it was written in an eighteenth-century Greek hand. Nevertheless, Smith did consult experts, so any conclusion that the manu-script may not be authentic must go beyond merely pointing out the inadequacies of the initial examination.[8] New reasons for doubting the apparent origin of the hand have to be developed.

There are three main reasons why the manuscript is unlikely to have been penned by an eighteenth-century monk at Mar Saba. First, the execution of the script raises questions of for-gery, including unnatural hesitations in the pen strokes, the "forger's tremor," and anomalies in the shape of the letters when compared with eighteenth-century manuscripts written at Mar Saba. Second, the manuscript's provenance cannot be traced back before 1958, which means that the opportunity for a twentieth-century origin cannot be ruled out. Third, there is another, previously unnoticed manuscript at Mar Saba from the same hand, which Smith himself identified as belonging to a named twentieth-century individual. Additional samples of that individual's Greek handwriting have been obtained and are found to account for the observed anomalies.

Forensic Questions of Forgery Raised by the Handwriting

Smith's approach of consulting only with Greek paleographers to authenticate the hand presumes that the best way to look for forgery is to detect anachronistic letter forms. While improperly formed letters are certainly one type of evidence used for detecting forgery, it is not the only or even the most conclusive evidence among experts in the forensic field of questioned document examination.[9] What is usually more critical is the line quality of the pen strokes. For example, one of the foremost authorities in this field, Albert S. Osborn, explains this as follows:

Forgeries nearly always show plainly the natural results of the strained circumstances described; too much attention is given to unimportant details and a slow, hesitating, and unnatural appearance is shown in the writing even when it is an accurate copy of the main features of the genuine writing imitated. Usually it is not even a good imitation of form characteristics and thus fails in the elementary part of the processes. The fundamental and usual defect in a forgery is, however, not divergence in form, but in a quality of line. . . . Close scrutiny of line quality alone often furnishes the basis for grave suspicion that a signature is not genuine.[10]

Unless highly practiced, forgers imitate the handwriting of their exemplars by drawing the letters rather than by writing them naturally. As a result, this difference is visible in the execution of the strokes as shaky lines, blunt ends, and pen lifts in the middle of strokes. These features do not exhibit a guilty mind, per se, because they sometimes can be attributed to the writer's age, fatigue, stress level, or other causes for a loss of fine motor control. However, they do signify that the writing was executed more slowly and deliberately than at a natural pace and makes handwriting purporting to be cursive or quickly written inherently deceptive. Even more suspicious than the forger's tremor is retouching. Forgers are often their own worst critics and few resist the temptation to patch up some of their poor strokes. Retouching requires fine motor control, so when the detailed patching of letters is found together with shaky or trembling lines, that tends to contradict age or stress as a contributing factor for the tremor.[11]

Figure 1 is an example of genuine and forged signatures of a person named Helen Huellen on disputed checks at issue in a jury trial at which Osborn had testified as an expert. The line quality of the two genuine signatures labeled "standard" is good. The strokes are written so rapidly that the pen is lifted off the page before the end of lines, resulting in pointed or "flying" ends. The large curves of the genuine signature are smoothly written in a single fluid stroke. By contrast, the forged samples are written more slowly: the pen comes to a complete stop at the end of each stroke, resulting in blunt ends (cf. at the ends of the letters *n*). The line quality of the disputed signature is shaky (in the letter *H*), an artifact known as the "forger's tremor." Another tell-tale indication of a slow deliberation while drawing letters is the presence of pen lifts in the middle of a stroke; even if the imitator is able to continue the line after a pen lift exactly on the natural curve, the ink often flows back into the previously drawn segment, creating a blob about twice the thickness of a line (cf. between the *e* and the *n* of *Helen*).[12]

Accordingly, it should be possible to tell if the hurried handwriting of *Theodore* is natural or simulated. Before examining the handwriting of *Theodore*, it is worthwhile to review what natural handwriting from Mar Saba in the eighteenth century looks like. Hundreds of manuscripts at Mar Saba were transferred to the Patriarchal Library in Jerusalem in 1865 (*Clement* 290), where they now form the Saba collection. In 1949–1950, Kenneth W. Clark visited Jerusalem, photographed many of these manuscripts, and deposited their microfilms in the Library of Congress.[13] Figures 2A–2C are samples of manuscripts in the Saba collection that Clark dated to the eighteenth century. More specifically, Figure 2A is obtained from an eighteenth-century *mathematarion* (Sabas 452, fol. 1R, line 11); Figure 2B is taken from a 1770 *sylloge* (Sabas 518, fol. 2R, line 5); and Figure 2C is from an eighteenth-century *sylloge* (Sabas 523, fol. 4R, lines 10–11). Each of these hands is different, but these instances show that they are written naturally. Many of the strokes terminate with flying ends, the curves are smoothly written, and the connections between letters do not feature pen lifts.

Figures 3A–3F are selections from the manuscript of *Theodore*, taken from Smith's photographs. Specifically, Figure 3A shows the first line of *Theodore* (I.1). The first character is what Smith termed a "sign of the cross" and is shown in detail in Figure 4A. Blunt ends at the beginnings and ends of the lines indicate that the strokes were written so slowly that the pen had come to a complete stop at the ends of the strokes. In *Theodore*, the pen had been on the paper even longer than that, since the ink continued to spread into the paper, leaving an ink blob. Many letters on this line of *Theodore* feature the blunt ends that evidence the writer's hesitation at the beginnings and ends of strokes, and the most egregious hesitations that resulted in ink blobs include the *tau* in τῶν, the *iota* in ἐπιστολῶν, the *tau* in the first τοῦ, the *omicron-upsilon* ligature at the end of ἁγιωτάτου, and the *sigma-tau* ligature (*stigma*) at the beginning of στρωματέως.

The next word is ἐκ (detail in Figure 4A) and it shows another tell-tale sign of forgery—the pen lift. More specifically, the line connecting the *epsilon* and the *kappa* shows evidence that it was written in two different strokes. First, the pen was lifted after the *epsilon* and the writer tried to continue the next stroke along the same course but the ink flowed back to the end of the first stroke, leaving a blob of ink in the middle of a stroke. This pen lift indicates that the writing here is a constructed imitation of a cursive hand, because a cursive writer would accomplish it in a single stroke. Other pen lifts on *Theodore* I.1 in unusual places are found on the stroke between the *omicron-upsilon* ligature and the circumflex accent in the first τοῦ, and the stroke connecting the *epsilon* and the *nu* in the word κλήμεντος.

The "forger's tremor" appears in the shaky quality of lines that should be smooth curves. In the first line of *Theodore*, the shakiness is evident in the *theta* of Θεοδώρω (detail in Figure 4B). Two of the *omicrons*, in ἐπιστολῶν and in Θεοδώρω are so shakily written as to appear square rather than circular. The tremor is also apparent in the long lines connecting the *omicron-upsilon* ligature and the circumflex accent in both the first and second τοῦ, in the *lambda* in κλήμεντος and the *mu* in στρωματέως.

A sign of retouching occurs in the *stigma* ligature at the beginning of the word στρωματέως. Instead of being distinctly written, there is a large blob of ink in the middle of the character as the result of overwriting an improperly written letter beneath it. Though the precise identity of the underlying letter cannot be determined, that letter was narrow, and it might have been an initial *sigma*.

The hand also shows a remarkable internal inconsistency in the very first line of *Theodore*, where the *tau* of the first τοῦ is short while the *tau* of the second τοῦ is tall. Overall in *Theodore*, the scribe shows a marked preference for a tall *tau* (which looks like a cursive American 7), except in the word τῶν where the short *tau* is necessary because of an interfering terminal abbreviation for the –ῶν. The one exception is in the very first opportunity to write a tall *tau*, which should have occurred in the first τοῦ. The inconsistently written *tau* is also interesting because the first stroke starts with a flying end, indicating some speed, but then pauses halfway in the middle of the letter and hesitates at the end, resulting in two large ink blobs (Figure 4C detail). The scribe's significant hesitation halfway through the erroneous stroke indicates that he just realized that he had written the wrong form of the *tau*.

The signs of deliberation and imitation continue throughout the writing of *Theodore*. Figure 3B is taken from *Theodore* I.4. The forger's tremor is manifest in the *delta* of the word (ὁ-)δοῦ, in the lines connecting the *alpha* and the smooth breathing of ἀπέρατον and ἄβυσσον, the *rho* of ἀπέρατον, the *beta* of ἄβυσ–σον, the squarish *omicron* near the end of πλανώμενοι, and the *mu* and *rho* in ἁμαρτιῶν. Ink blobs betraying hesitation can be seen at the beginning of the *upsilon* in (ὁ-)δοῦ, for the *nu* of ἀπέρατον, the first *sigma* of ἄβυσσον, the *tau* of τῶν, the *nu* of σαρκικῶν. Pen lifts are evident in the middle of the *rho* of ἀπέρατον, between the *alpha* and the *tau* in ἐνσωμάτων. The word (ὁ-)δοῦ on *Theodore* I.4 is also noteworthy in that it is the only instance in the manuscript in which the scribe failed to use a ligature for *omicron-upsilon* pair.

In Figure 3C from *Theodore* I.7, the writer is beginning to show some comfort in the hand but continues to exhibit signs of deliberation in drawing the letters, though blunt ends are evident, for example, at the end of the first *upsilon* in ἐλευθέρους, and at the *nu* and the second *iota* in εἶναι. Nevertheless, the tremor is still present in the *theta* and *rho* of ἐλευθέρους, in the first four letters of δοῦλοι, in both *gammas* of γεγόνασιν, and in the *theta* of ἐπιθυμιῶν. Unnatural pen lifts in the middle of what should be smooth curves can be seen in the left leg of the *lambda* in δοῦλοι, between the *epsilon* and *gamma* of γεγόνασιν, and between the *pi* and the *epsilon* of ἐπιθυμιῶν. Despite the apparent speed of writing that the cursive might indicate, the scribe had enough time to go back and retouch some of the letters. For example, the *lambda* of δοῦλοι, however, shows a lot of retouching and the letter still looks poor. The scribe also managed to remember to use a ligature for the *omicron-upsilon* in δοῦλοι, in contrast to the word (ὁ-)δοῦ at the beginning of *Theodore* I. 4 (Figure 3B).

By the middle of the second page, *Theodore* II.18, shown in Figure 3D, the letters are more quickly written, with more flying ends, yet blunt ends are still found throughout and ink blobs at the *taus* in the two instances of τοῦ. Nevertheless, the forger's tremor is still evident in the *iota* of ἐκεῖ and the *theta* of ἐλευθερία. Both abbreviated instances of κυρίου show pen lifts between the initial *kappa* and the final *omicron-upsilon* ligature, as well as between the *epsilon* and the *upsilon* in ἐλευθερία. The scribe also has taken the time to retouch the end of the *tau* in the word τό.

Figure 3E is the last line of the second page (*Theod.* II.26), and the hand is showing more fluidity. The number of ink blobs at the ends of lines is reduced over the previous lines, though a few still remain, e.g., at the beginning of both *mus* in μνημεῖον, and at the beginning of the letter *kappa* in καὶ. The scribe still manifests a tremor in the letter *theta*, here in the word ἀπῆλθεν. In the next word, μετ᾽, there are two pen lifts on the connecting line between the *epsilon* and *tau*, which may have been added later in retouching.

The final line of *Theodore* is shown in Figure 3F. Except for the first few words, the writing is noticeably more fluid (e.g., φιλοσοφίαν ἐξήγησις). Even the first *theta* of ἀληθῆ shows less shakiness than before, although the tremor returns in the *theta* of ἀληθῆ and in the square-like *omicron* of φιλοσοφίαν. The left leg of the two-stroke *lambda* in ἀληθὴς is written deliberately, as evidenced by the large blobs of ink at both ends, while the *lambda* in the following ἀληθῆ shows more competence, being written in a single stroke hook terminating with a flying end.

The pervasiveness of these signs of simulation in a document ostensibly executed in a rapid cursive raises the specter that *Theodore* is a drawn imitation of an eighteenth-century hand. The tremor and blunt ends show that the strokes are written slowly, and the pen lifts and retouching indicate that the strokes are written deliberately. The decision to employ cursive handwriting is a trade-off between legibility and speed. In the case of *Theodore*, the choice of a cursive hand for such a slow and deliberate writer is hard to explain. Neither legibility nor speed resulted from the decision, but the intrinsic variation of cursive handwriting helps to mask execution errors.

While innocent explanations could individually account for some features, such as the tremor, they are difficult to reconcile with all the features of the hand. For example, a writer's advanced age can be responsible for the presence of a tremor in the execution of the hand, but the tremor caused by advanced age precludes the fine motor control as evidenced by the retouching of the strokes between letters. It is likewise difficult to credit stress for the cause of the poor line quality. Fear of being caught copying a scandalous text is belied by the writer's lack of haste in retouching various letters and in neatly justifying the margins. If an increasing awareness of *Theodore*'s content troubling to an orthodox monk was a cause of stress, then the scribe's unease with writing should increase throughout the text, not decrease. Fatigue could produce an uneven concentration of poor line quality, but the orthographic anomalies and lack of confidence with the hand tend to be concentrated toward the beginning of the document and taper off toward the end, while the effects of fatigue should be the opposite.

The prospect that *Theodore* is an imitation, as indicated by the forensic examination of the quality of the scribe's strokes, is reinforced paleographically by the anomalies in the shapes and forms of the letters. For example, the formation of the letter *lambda* in the Mar Saba collection is written with two strokes, with the left leg intersecting the right leg near the top.[14] The *lambda* in *Theodore*, on the other hand, is formed in two different ways. One way is a single-stroke "hook" *lambda*, with the left leg being connected to the bottom of the right leg.[15] There is also a two-stroke *lambda* in *Theodore*, but, unlike those in the referenced Mar Saba manuscripts, its left leg intersects near the bottom of the right leg.[16] Another instance is in the shape of the short *tau*. The short *tau* in *Theodore* is usually written in a single stroke,[17] but the short *tau* at Mar Saba is written with two strokes.[18]

The use of the standard *nomina sacra* abbreviations for Jesus, Christ, Lord, God, and other holy words in *Theodore* is also unusual for its purported origin. *Theodore* consistently uses the *nomina sacra* for Lord and man, but not for Jesus and David. For example, Figure 3D twice shows an abbreviation for κυρίου as κ(υρι)ου, while Figure 3E does not abbreviate᾽ Ἰησοῦς. Now, the *nomina sacra* gradually fell into disuse starting in the eighteenth century, but the *nomen sacrum* of Jesus was still in use in many documents at Mar Saba in the eighteenth century, particularly when other *nomina sacra* were also employed, as shown in Figure 2C. Another difference in the way the *nomina sacra* were employed in *Theodore* as compared with the referenced Mar Saba manuscripts is that the genitive case of the *nomina sacra* ends with an *omicron-upsilon* ligature (Figure 3D), not with a plain *upsilon* (Figure 2C).

Other aspects of the manuscript are anomalous when compared with the known Mar Saba manuscripts. One peculiarity is the sign of the cross, from which Smith inferred that the writer was a Greek monk (*Clement* 2), but other manuscripts from Mar Saba do not evidence this feature. A conceivable interpretation of the character is that it is a dagger or obelisk, which is a text-critical sign that signifies a spurious text.

Another peculiarity is the type of pen. The manuscripts in the Mar Saba collection show the use of a quill pen with a fairly wide nib, even for smaller sized annotations. The nib of the pen used to write *Theodore*, on the other hand, is   much narrower, almost point-sized. Another visible difference between *Theodore* and the previous Mar Saba samples is that the ink tends more readily to spread through the paper of *Theodore*. This is not due to Smith's photography as some have protested,[19] but the usual result of using ink on very old paper. When paper is made, manufacturers add sizing to the surface of the paper to prevent the ink from spreading. Over time, the sizing is lost and the paper begins to act more like blotting paper. Exposure to conditions of dampness or mildew are the most significant culprits.[20] Both fuzzy lines and large blobs of ink are evident in the manuscript of *Theodore*, and they are most pronounced on the first line of each page near the top margin (e.g., I.1 in Figure 3A). Clearly then, *Theodore* was written on very old, absorbent paper.

Without the physical manuscript, however, it is difficult to determine whether the spreading of the ink reflects being written on a hundred-year old paper, if genuine, or on three-hundred year old paper, if a modern fake. Indeed, the unavailability of the manuscript renders further consideration of the paper, pen, and ink admittedly speculative, but the photographs can suggest some avenues of investigation should the manuscript ever be found again.

For example, Scott G. Brown noticed the edges of the paper have been browned, acknowledging that "[t]his is normally an indication that the book had been shelved for long periods in places where sunlight could irradiate onto the edges of the paper, which is not likely to have occurred in the dark tower library at Mar Saba."[21] Nevertheless Brown was reluctant to reach this normal conclusion because the lighting conditions and the film quality for the photographs were unknown.[22] Less sensitive to lighting conditions, however, is the fuzziness of the lines due to the absorbency of the paper. The lines are noticeably more fuzzy near the edges of the page, suggesting that the paper is more absorbent near the edges, and thus the book was not only exposed to sunlight but also to dampness. Indeed, mold or water stains are visible in the color photographs published by Hedrick of the first page of *Theodore* and of the first extant page of the book.[23] Dampness is also not likely to be a factor at the desert monastery library. Unfortunately, Smith did not publish any photographs of the first extant page; the margins of the photographs in *Clement* are cropped, and the only, non-cropped photograph of the first page of *Theodore* (*Secret Gospel* 38) has a black-and-white cord obscuring the place where the stain was visible in later photographs.

As another example, the ink looks anomalous from the photographs. The ink used at Mar Saba, as evidenced in some of the manuscripts, is sometimes so caustic as to scorch the opposite pages of the book or pass through the page itself. This may indicate that iron-gall ink was in use at Mar Saba, which can be made from about four ingredients.[24] No such corrosion on the opposite pages of *Theodore* can be seen in the photographs. Either the ink formulation used to write *Theodore* is less caustic than that used at Mar Saba in the 1700s, or the ink had been applied to the book for a shorter time. Neither possibility favors the authenticity of the manuscript, but this line of questioning can only be settled with the physical examination of the manuscript to determine if the ink really was an iron-gall ink.

The unavailability of ink for testing means that Brown was overconfident in concluding that the ink used to write

Theodore was an iron-gall ink solely because it appeared "rusty brown" in the color photographs (the ink actually appears darker to me).[25] Color alone cannot identify an ink, especially from photographs taken under uncertain conditions. Yet Brown considered this fact significant because it takes from a quarter century to a century for an iron gall ink, to turn from black to rusty brown, depending on its formulation and the amount of ink that was deposited, which can be accelerated under poor storage conditions.[26] But the color of the ink in the later photographs tells us nothing: they were taken twenty years *after* Smith photographed the letter, and it is impossible to tell what color the ink was in Smith's black-and-white photographs.[27] Also inconclusive is the color of the paper, which Brown argued became brown due to the iron-gall ink.[28] However, the paper is lighter, not darker, near the ink. Moreover, the paper immediately surrounding the ink has the same deep yellow color as that of the blank endpapers of my personal copy of the Voss edition. There is no dispute that the paper on which *Theodore* was written is about 350 years old.

Accordingly, a detailed examination of the way in which the document was written raises a substantial question about the genuineness of the handwriting. The indications of hesitations, tremors, and retouching of letters indicate that its apparently hurried cursive was executed more slowly than it purports to be. The orthographic errors and anomalous letter forms indicate that its writer had not fully mastered the style of handwriting. Though a physical examination of the manuscript, its papers, and its ink might be able to place the origin of the document outside of the capability of twentieth-century fakers, none has yet been performed nor will be any time soon.

No Trace of the Manuscript before 1958

A solid provenance goes a long distance in resolving any residual doubts about the authenticity of an artifact, while a weak provenance can only magnify the problems that a questioned document may bear. The *editio princeps* for *Secret Mark* presents a rather negative but truthful assessment of the evidence for the manuscript's origins: "Thus we have, in the last analysis, no *proof* that the present text was or was not copied in Mar Saba, or that the MS from which it was copied was or was not in the Mar Saba library" (*Clement* 290, emphasis original). In fact, there is no proof that the manuscript or even the book was present at Mar Saba prior to Smith's second visit in 1958.

There is no direct evidence requiring the manuscript to have been written before 1958. Strictly speaking, the manuscript of *Secret Mark* itself is modern. The Clementine letter quoting *Secret Mark* is not extant in any ancient or medieval medium; it was written on a modern-era medium, a book published in 1646 and still available on the used book market. As Donald Akenson had noticed, "if the item was the product of a forger, he was engaged in the relatively easy task of obtaining a printed book and of using inks and handwritings that are accessible at the present day, quite a different task from forging an ancient document."[29] In 1975, Quesnell pointed out that "[p]ossession of a copy of the 1646 edition of Voss Ignatius poses no problem,"[30] and even today the Voss edition is obtainable in the used book market: one copy of the 1646 edition had been offered for sale in December 2003 for €280 (about U.S. $320).[31] In addition, Smith noted no ownership or other marks of provenance in the book, and the most probable places for such information, the front cover and first pages, had been destroyed (*Secret Gospel* 13).

As for direct, external evidence of the book's earlier existence at Mar Saba, Smith did not present any catalog information, even though Smith perused a 1910 catalog of "191 titles . . . written without comments."[32] The 1910 catalog's bare listing would not have documented the existence of the handwritten addition, but Smith's failure to preserve any information about the book's prior presence at Mar Saba is unsettling. Smith claimed that he "did not have the time to study it,"[33] yet

Smith certainly did have the time to examine the catalog to ascertain that it contained 191 titles and no comments. Smith could have photographed the catalog, which is how he preserved evidence for *Secret Mark* and the other manuscripts he examined at Mar Saba. At the very least, Smith, who had been "walking on air" just a few days earlier over this text, could have specifically looked for the Voss edition as being among its 191 titles and documented at least that much about the contents of the 1910 catalog. Instead, Smith argued that the mere fact of a book's not being in a catalog proves nothing (*Clement* 290). The most rational inference from Smith's behavior is the one that Quesnell drew: the 1910 catalog did not contain the Voss edition in which *Secret Mark* was written.[34]

The library of Mar Saba was not a secure archive, and its physical security was sufficiently lax to involve several thefts as well as the appearance of new materials.[35] For example, in the spring of 1976, Guy Stroumsa was informed that "most books from the monastery's library had been moved to the Patriarchate library, after too many thefts had occurred."[36] Furthermore, security at Mar Saba would have been more concerned about books being removed from its library than about books being smuggled into it. The book is not difficult to conceal due to its small dimensions (approximately 15 cm x 20 cm or 6" x 7 3/4").[37] Though there is some debate about whether the conditions at Mar Saba would have precluded someone from copying the text into an existing book there, the feasibility of smuggling means that *Secret Mark* need not have actually been written at Mar Saba.[38]

The lack of direct confirmation for the manuscript's existence at Mar Saba before 1958 means that corroborating the prior presence of *Secret Mark* can only be done indirectly—that is, by assessing whether the book in which *Secret Mark* was found is consistent with those printed books that were present at Mar Saba in the 1700s. However, by all accounts, the number of printed books of that age at Mar Saba is small. When

Robert Curzon, Jr., visited Mar Saba in the 1830s, he noted that the tower library at Mar Saba contained "about a thousand books, almost all manuscripts, but the whole of them were works of divinity."[39] Without the 1910 catalog, Smith's survey of the library in 1958 remains the most accessible source for getting a sense of what kinds of old printed books at Mar Saba bore manuscript material. In all, he identified ten such printed books, which are listed below along with Smith's inventory number:

No. 6   ʿΙερῶν Λειτουργιῶν (Venice, 1805)

No. 11   Εὐχολογίου (Venice, 1711)

No. 15   Βιβλίου ὀνομαζόμενον Θησαυρός (Venice, 1628)

No. 20   Βιβλίου ὀνομαζόμενον Θησαυρός (Venice, 1628)

No. 21   Εὐχαί τοῦ λυχνικοῦ καὶ τοῦ῀ Ορθρου (Venice, 1746)

No. 22   ʿΗ Καλοκαιρινή (Venice, 1656)

No. 23   Ψαλτηρίου (Venice, 1760)

No. 26   Συνταγματίου (Venice, 1682)

No. 48   Εὐχῶν τοῦ λυχνικοῦ καὶ τοῦ῀ Ορθρου (Venice, 1782)

No. 65   *Epistolae genuinae S. Ignatii Martyriis* (Amsterdam, 1646).

The book containing *Secret Mark*, no. 65, sticks out like a sore thumb. It is the only book printed in Amsterdam; all the others were published in Venice. The most that Smith could do to link the book to Venice is to suggest that its "heavy, white paperboard" binding was common in Venice (*Clement* 1), but paperboard binding was also common throughout Europe in the seventeenth century.[40] My own personal copy of the same 1646 edition of this book also has a heavy, white paperboard binding, yet it was bound in England. Further complicating Smith's implied link to Venice was that, by 1684, it had been placed on the *Index Librorum Prohibitorum* and censored in Catholic Europe because it was published by Protestants in their polemics on the authority of bishops.

While this censorship had no jurisdiction over Mar Saba, it would have limited the opportunities for the book to pass through Venice from Amsterdam on its way to Mar Saba.

The subject matter of the Voss edition also differs from that of the other books. The other books comprise liturgical, devotional, and administrative material, but no. 65 is the only printed book in Smith's catalog encompassing patristics.[41] Also different is the language of the book. Smith's no. 65 is the only book with a Latin title and the facing Latin translation of the Greek would not have been useful for the Greek Orthodox monks. In fact, the presence of any Latin text at Mar Saba would have been remarkable as Smith did not document any other Latin text in his 1960 catalog. Even more unusual for its presence at an Eastern Orthodox monastery is the sectarian nature of the book. The Amsterdam edition was prepared for controversy between Protestants and Catholics—a controversy that was not raging in Eastern Orthodoxy.

If the only evidence that the book existed at Mar Saba prior to 1958 is Smith's word, this brings up a sensitive issue. Great care must be taken before calling a scholar's integrity into question, and accusations of a scholar making intentional falsehoods to the academy should be based on compelling evidence.[42] Fortunately, this unpleasant task is unnecessary because Smith's publications did not unequivocally assert that the manuscript had been present at Mar Saba before his second visit there. For example, Smith wrote in *Clement* about *Secret Mark*:

> The manuscripts of Mar Saba proved, on examination, mostly modern. This was no surprise, since it is well known that the rich collection of ancient manuscripts for which the monastery was famous in the early nineteenth century, had been transferred to Jerusalem for safekeeping in the eighteen-sixties. Little seems to have been left behind at that time except scraps and printed books. But in subsequent years there has been a gradual accumulation of other manu-

> script material, both new and old. During my stay I was able
> to examine, label, and describe some seventy items. . . .[43]
> Among the items examined was one, number 65 in my pub-
> lished notes, of which the manuscript element consisted of
> two and a half pages of writing at the back of an old printed
> book. (*Clement* ix)

According to Smith, he "examined" the manuscript at Mar
Saba and the manuscript was among the items he was able to
"examine, label, and describe." Smith's assertion does not
mean that either the manuscript in the book, or even the book
itself, was present at Mar Saba prior to his visit in the summer
of 1958. The catalog that Smith published in 1960 is no more
helpful: he merely stated that its 76 items "are found"
(εὑρίσκονται, present tense) in the library or the tower, a statement that was technically true when the catalog was published
after his stay.[44]

Smith's other possible claims of discovery were carefully
guarded by conditionals. For example, Smith wrote: "If the letter was really by Clement I had a discovery of extraordinary
importance" (*Secret Gospel* 18).[45] On the other hand, if the letter was not really by Clement, then Smith need not have had
a discovery at all. The authenticity of *Secret Mark*, therefore,
does not affect the logical truth of his implication.

Smith's guarded language about how he came across *Secret
Mark* is particularly intriguing because he showed no such reticence in claiming to have discovered other written materials
at Mar Saba. In his popular account, Smith wrote in reference
to fragments of Sophocles's *Ajax*, "I also found that much older
manuscript material had been used for bookbinding" (*Secret
Gospel* 12); and for a manuscript of pseudo-Macarius, "I came
on an old binding so far gone to pieces that I could get out the
'boards' around which the leather had been sewn" (*Secret
Gospel* 13). By contrast, his account of *Secret Mark* is much less
explicit, stating only that he found himself: "Then, one after-
noon near the end of my stay, *I found myself in my cell*, staring

incredulously at a text written in a tiny scrawl I had not even tried to read in the tower when I picked out the book containing it" (*Secret Gospel* 12, emphasis added). Smith's reluctance to claim credit for finding *Secret Mark* but not for other texts is not only telling but also helps to resolve his ambiguous statement of a "discovery of a manuscript (which I found in 1958 at the Monastery of Mar Saba in the Judean desert)" (*Secret Gospel* ix). Based on Smith's explicit language, that statement refers to either of the two manuscripts he actually claimed to find—not to *Secret Mark*.

Arguably, these statements could have been written before Smith felt accused of forgery and needed to be more explicit as to the manuscript's origins. Such an explanation would have been less applicable by the time of Smith's response to Quesnell, yet his statements remained coy. For example, Smith's reply to Quesnell, "I left the MS in the Mar Saba library and have no information as to what has been done with it,"[46] does not quite assert that he found it there and can even be construed as admitting to his depositing it there. As another example, Smith stated, "Nothing I saw in the MS, nor anything seen in the photographs by other scholars, raised any suspicion that the text was modern."[47] This statement does not manage to encompass those suspicions of modernity arising from his personal knowledge of the manuscript's origins apart from his visible inspection of the handiwork. Even Smith's defense against being the forger left room to maneuver: "Quesnell insinuates that I forged the MS. Such accusations are customary when important MSS are discovered. Denial does not dispose of them; anyone who would forge a manuscript would deny that he had done so."[48] This "non-denial denial" did not disavow being the forger but merely digressed about why a denial would not be satisfactory.[49]

In short, the evidence, even in Smith's publications disclosing *Secret Mark* to the world, does not support the manuscript's existence at Mar Saba any earlier than 1958. Indeed, the book with its manuscript could have been introduced into the Mar Saba at any time up to and including Smith's second visit to Mar Saba. Coupled with the forensic indications of forgery in the execution of the hand, the poverty of the manuscript's provenance means that the document could well be a fake as recent as 1958.

Evidence from Smith's Hand Identifying the Scribe

Although the evidence adduced so far raises the possibility that the manuscript is a modern fake, it does not establish when or by whom the manuscript was written. Fortunately, this information has not been lost, because Smith's writings contain previously unnoticed evidence that answers this question.

Theodore is not the only manuscript from Mar Saba that Smith photographed and published. Smith published photographs of two other manuscripts in a 1960 article in *Archaeology*.[50] The first is a fifteenth-century manuscript of Sophocles's *Ajax* that was used to bind a prayer book printed in 1746 and was assigned no. 21 in Smith's catalog.[51] The other is a more recent Greek manuscript, no. 22, whose binding contains several older manuscript pages pasted together, including those from medieval Georgian, Arabic, and Greek manuscripts.[52] The same photograph of manuscript no. 22 was reproduced on page 37 of Smith's *Secret Gospel* and is partially shown here in Figure 5A.

Three different handwriting styles are found on the page facing the pasted end-papers and shown on the right side of the photograph of manuscript no. 22. The first of the hands is at the top of the first recto page (detailed in Figure 5B) and, in its shaping of the letters *tau*, *pi*, *rho*, and the *omicron-upsilon* ligature, resembles the hand of *Theodore*. The first hand also resembles *Theodore* in its choice of a narrow nib, while the other hands on the page use the wider pen nib more favored at Mar Saba in the eighteenth century. In addition, the first hand also shows the blunt ends and the "forger's tremor" indicative of the

person who penned *Theodore*. For these reasons, whoever wrote
Theodore was also the first hand of manuscript no. 22.

The information Smith disclosed about the hands in manuscript no. 22 is significant. Interestingly, Smith's catalog entry
did not date the first hand to the eighteenth century, but to the
twentieth century:

> The present book in our catalog includes not just an exam-
> ple of a completed manuscript (of which the library contains
> rather much), but also for this reason it is particularly rich in
> notes by previous owners or users: f. 1 r., M. Madiotes (hand-
> writing of the 20th cen.). The monk Dionysios, Archiman-
> drite, (handwriting of the 19th cen.): . . . Anobos monk of
> the Holy Sepulcher (18th cen.?). . . .⁵³

According to Smith, manuscript no. 22 is important not
only because it contains many samples of handwriting, but
also because it contains information about the people who
wrote them. For the first hand, even though it resembles an
eighteenth-century style, Smith confidently dated it to the
twentieth century and attributed it to a certain M. Madiotes
(M. Μαδιότης). This person lacks a religious title and for that
reason appears to be a visitor to Mar Saba. While the name
superficially appears Greek with the –ότης suffix of many
Greek surnames, such a surname cannot be found at all in the
current Greek telephone directory available online. Rather,
the name is a pseudonym built on the root μαδ–. Few modern
Greek words begin with μαδ–, but one of them is the verb
μαδώ, which literally means "to lose hair" and has a figurative
meaning of "to swindle."⁵⁴

Smith has thus preserved a lot more information about the
person who penned *Theodore* than previously realized. This
person belongs to the twentieth century, this person is not a
Greek orthodox monk, this person had a given name beginning with the letter M, and this person bore a pseudonymous
surname that means either "baldy" or "swindler." This person
bears an uncanny resemblance to Morton Smith himself. After

all, Smith belonged to the twentieth century, Smith was not a Greek orthodox monk, Smith's given name starts with the letter M, and Smith was substantially bald well before 1960.[55]

If Smith actually penned the manuscript, many of his other remarkable conclusions about the scribe based on the handwriting describe himself. For example, Smith claimed that the scribe was "an experienced writer and a scholar" (Clement 1). So was Smith. Also Smith deduced that the scribe's "handwriting had been influenced by his study of patristics texts in western editions" (3). Smith had studied patristics texts in western editions. Smith further concluded that the writer "was interested not only in patristics, but also in the beginnings of western critical scholarship," (3) a judgment true for Smith as well. Quesnell was justifiably suspicious because Smith's conclusions about the scribe that he apparently derived from the handwriting were "completely unsupported" and "too loosely drawn,"[56] but, if Smith was the scribe, Smith's conclusions were more factually supported than they had appeared to Quesnell.

If this is a cleverly disguised confession claiming credit for penning the Secret Mark manuscript, it is still important to probe whether it is a false confession. Smith certainly had expertise in eighteenth-century handwriting. In 1951–1952, Smith visited libraries in Greece, photographed many manuscripts written in the 1700s, and specifically commented in print on seventeen such Greek manuscripts.[57] One of the libraries in Dimistana he visited contained over sixty Greek manuscripts written in the eighteenth century.[58] Despite the complexity of the handwriting from that period with its heavy use of abbreviations and ligatures, Smith demonstrated competence in reading, transcribing, and dating these manuscripts. Smith did not lose this expertise just six years later when it came time to inspect the Secret Mark manuscript. He read and provisionally dated the hand before discussing the text with Scholem in Jerusalem and deciding to obtain additional paleo-

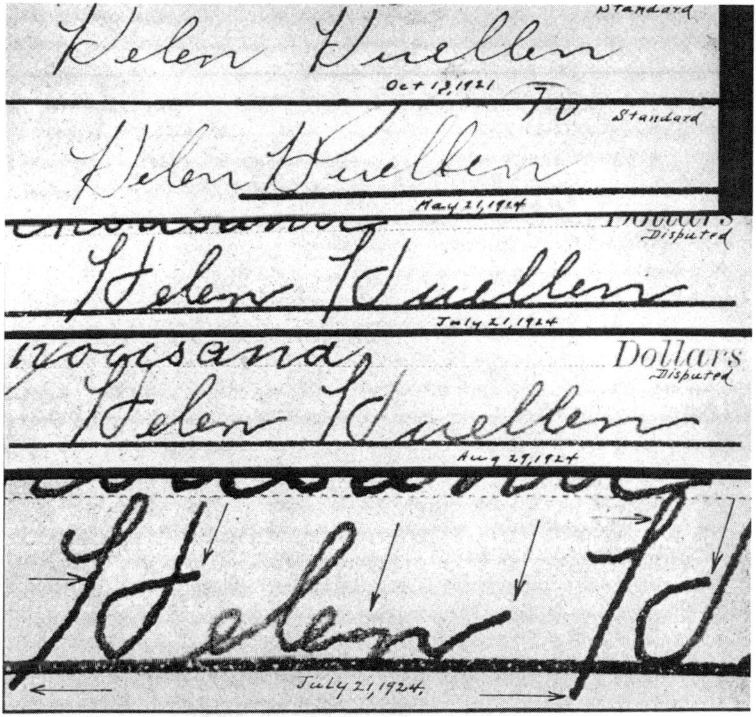

Figure 1: Osborn Exhibit

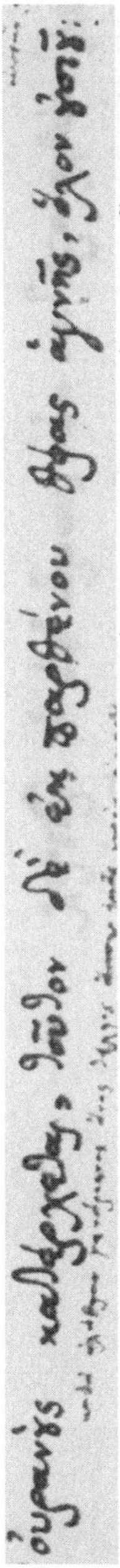

οὐρανοὺς κατέρχεται τοῦτον δὲ ἐκ παρθένου θείας ἁγνῆς ὅλον οὐσιοῦ

Figure 2A: *Sabas 452, fol. 1R, line 11 (18th cen.)*

ψυχὴν τοῦ δούλου σου σῶτερ ἀνάπαυσον φιλάττων

Figure 2B: *Sabas 518, fol. 2R, line 5 (1770)*

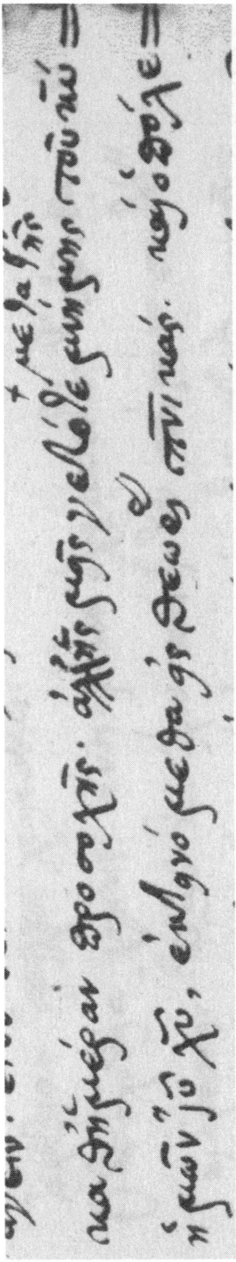

καθ᾽ ἡμέραν προσοχῆς ἀλλ᾽ ἧς μεῖς γε τότε μνήμης τοῦ κυ
ἡμῶν ιυ χυ ἐκτεινόμεθα εἰς θεωρίας πνικάς καὶ ὁ πόλε

Figure 2C: *Sabas 523, fol. 4R, line 10–11 (18th cen.)*

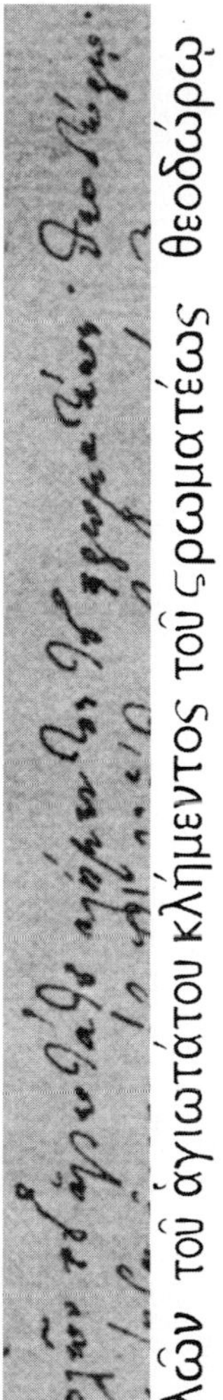

ἐκ τῶν ἐπιστολῶν τοῦ ἁγιωτάτου κλήμεντος τοῦ ςρωμάτεως θεοδώρῳ

Figure 3A: Theodore I.1

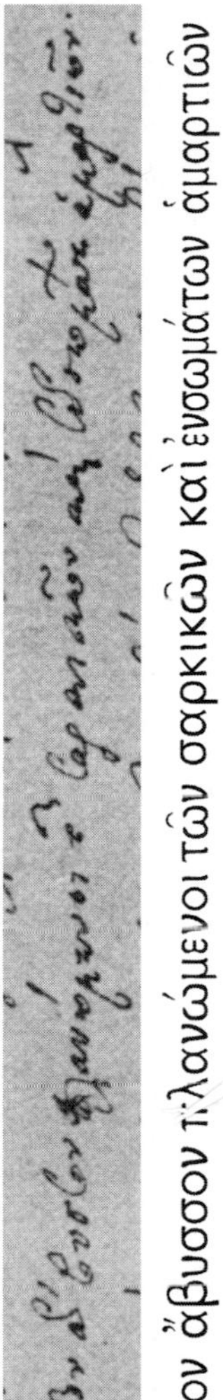

δοῦ εἰς ἀπέρατον ἄβυσσον τ λανώμενοι τῶν σαρκικῶν καὶ ἐνσωμάτων ἁμαρτιῶν

Figure 3B: Theodore I.4

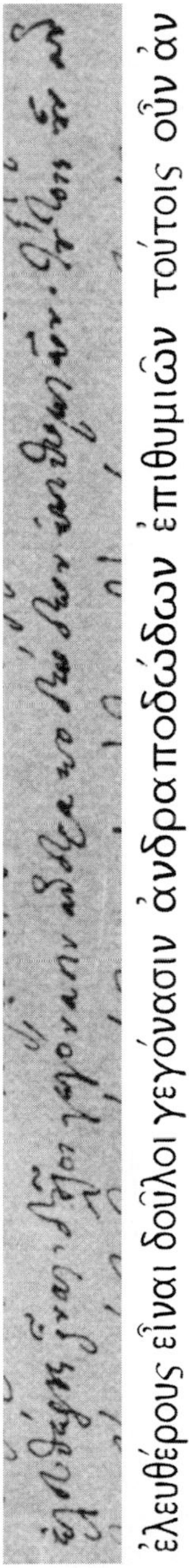

ἐλευθέρους εἶναι δοῦλοι γεγόνασιν ἀνδραποδώδων ἐπιθυμιῶν τούτοις οὖν ἂν

Figure 3C: Theodore I.7

τοῦ κοῦ οὗ δὲ τὸ πνεῦμα τοῦ κου φησίν ἐκεῖ ἐλευθερία πάντα γάρ καὶ

Figure 3D: Theodore II.18

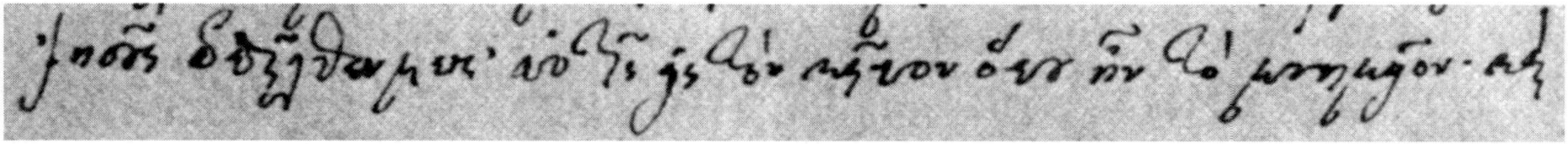

ἰησοῦς ἀπῆλθεν μετ' αὐτῆς εἰς τὸν κῆπον ὅπου ἦν τὸ μνημεῖον καὶ

Figure 3E: Theodore II.26

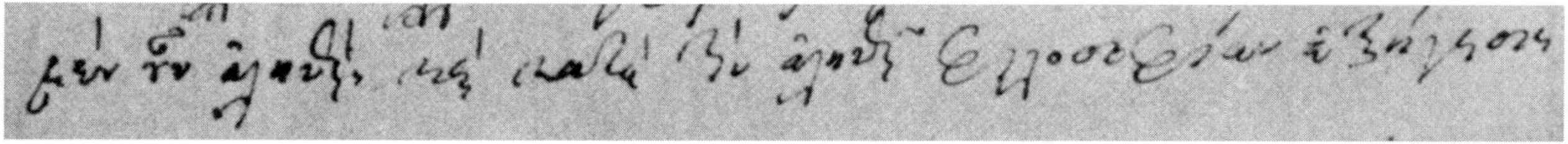

μὲν οὖν ἀληθῆς καὶ κατὰ τὴν ἀληθῆ φιλοσοφίαν ἐξήγησις

Figure 3F: Theodore III.18

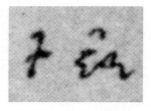

Figure 4A: Theodore I.1 (Detail)

Figure 4B. Theodore I.1 (Detail)

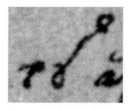

Figure 4C: Theodore I.1 (Detail)

Figure 5A: Smith, Mar Saba 22

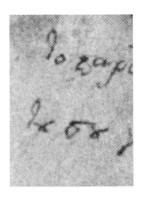

Figure 5B: Smith, Mar Saba 22 (Detail)

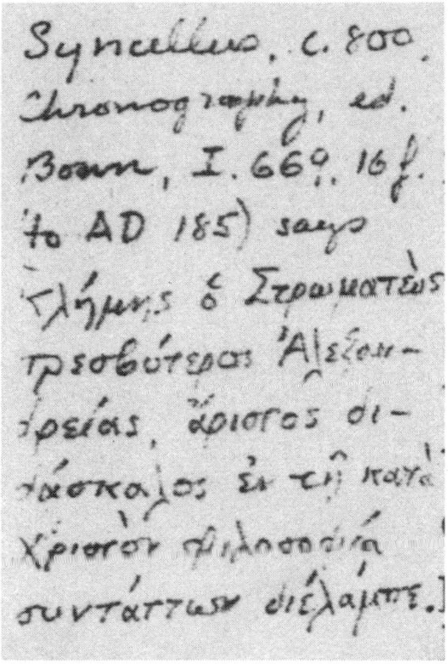

Syncellus, c. 800.
Chronography, ed.
Bonn, I. 669. 16 f.
(to AD 185) says
Κλήμης ὁ Στρωματεὺς
πρεσβύτερος Ἀλεξαν-
δρείας, ἄριστος δι-
δάσκαλος ἐν τῇ κατὰ
Χριστὸν φιλοσοφίᾳ
συντάττων διέλαμπε.]

Figure 6A: *Smith*, *Smith* scholium, *p. XVI*

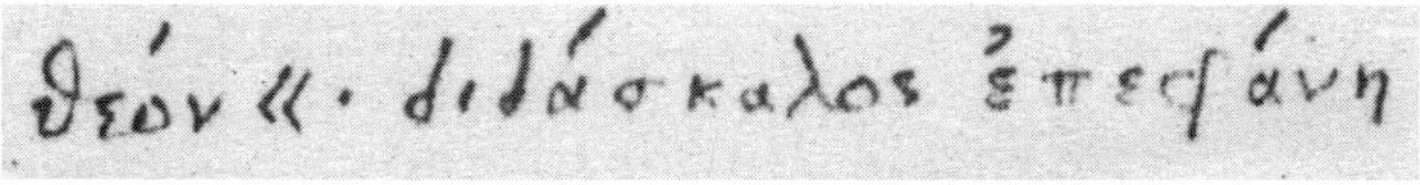

θεὸν «. διδάσκαλος ἐπεφάνη

Figure 6B: *Smith*, *Smith* scholium, *p.* 7

	θ		λ		τ	
Sabas 452 fol. 1R						
Sabas 518 fol. 2R						
Sabas 523 fol. 4R						
Sabas 574 fol. 1R						
Sabas 591 fol. 1R						
Sabas 648 fol. 1V						
Sabas 649 fol. 1R						
Theodore fol. 1V						
Morton Smith						

Figure 7

graphical opinions in Athens and on his return to the United States (*Secret Gospel* 18–21).

Smith's familiarity with Western-style Greek handwriting may clear up another puzzle in the hand of the *Theodore*. One of Smith's colleagues noticed that the hand shows a distinctly Western appearance (*Clement* 2). While Smith is undoubtedly correct that this does not "prove" that the scribe was from the Western part of Greece (i.e. the Greek mainland, since many Greeks then were still residing in what is now Turkey), it conflicts with the Eastern location of Mar Saba. Smith's suggestion of the influence of Western typography in printed books is possible, as is the scribe's having learned the hand from exemplars in the Western part of Greece. In fact, the sample autograph presented by Smith of a similar hand of Patriarch Callinicus III illustrates this point, because, as Smith did not tell us, Callinicus was himself a Western Greek.[59] Both possible Western influences on the hand apply to Smith.

Smith also had the resources to obtain the manuscript material, and he even admitted his prior familiarity with the book: "Voss's work on Ignatius had been published many times, I knew, but it occurred to me that I could date the edition by photographing the first and last preserved pages and comparing them with complete volumes, so I took those" (*Secret Gospel* 13). As mentioned, copies of the Voss edition are still being sold today for about $320. But back in the 1950s, it would have sold for less, and a copy missing its front cover and first page should have cost much less. Smith's financial status as a life-long bachelor meant that he was relatively more able to afford such a book, even on a professor's salary. In fact, Smith was an avid book collector and had amassed a library of 10,000 volumes by the time of his death in 1991.[60]

Smith bequeathed his library to the Jewish Theological Seminary in New York City, which became the Morton Smith Collection.[61] This collection includes not only a 1935 book discussing eighteenth-century Greek handwriting,[62] but also

Smith's personal copy of Otto Stählin's four-volume critical edition of the surviving works of Clement of Alexandria. The first three volumes are in hardcover and were purchased from a used bookstore in England, but both parts of Stählin's index for the fourth volume, which includes a full concordance of Clement's vocabulary, are in paperback. Although the fourth volume is almost entirely clean of his annotations, the first three volumes of Stählin's edition of Clement in the Morton Smith Collection are heavily annotated. (Smith often scribbled notes in his books and has thus left a legacy of his own handwriting in Greek.) Figures 6A and 6B are samples of Smith's undated notes, photocopied from pages xvi and 7, respectively, from the first volume of Smith's personal copy of Stählin's edition.[63]

Of course, Smith's normal Greek handwriting was not an eighteenth-century hand, and one would not usually expect to match an imitator's own natural handwriting with the imitation. Nevertheless, it occasionally happens that the imitators lapse back into their usual hand.[64] As explained above, a major anomaly in the formation of the letters in *Theodore* when compared with manuscripts written at Mar Saba is the one-stroke "hook" *lambda* in free variation with a two-stroke *lambda*. For both forms of the letter, the left leg intersects the right leg near the bottom. These forms are strikingly different from the manuscripts written at Mar Saba, which consistently employ a two-stroke *lambda* with the left leg intersecting very high up on the right leg. In the first sample of Smith's writing reproduced in Figure 5A, Smith alternated between a single-stroke (in' Ἀλεξανδρείας, διδάσκαλος) and a two-stroke *lambda* with a low left leg (in Κλήμης, φιλοσοφία, and διέλαμπε). Smith's own handwriting not only happens to explain the unusual single-stroke hook *lambda* in *Theodore* and the unusual two-stroke *lambda* with a low left leg, but also the free variation between these unusual forms.

As another example, the one-stroke short *tau* was used in *Theodore* but not in the Mar Saba manuscripts of the eighteenth century, which use a two-stroke short *tau* instead. The one-stroke short *tau* also happens to be found in nearly every *tau* throughout the sample depicted in Figure 5A.[65] Yet another example is the shape of the *theta*. The *thetas* of *Theodore* in Figures 3A–3F and the Smith *scholium* of Figure 6B are very similar, including a leading horizontal stroke at midline. The writers of the Mar Saba manuscripts in Figures 2A and 2C, on the other hand, do not show this commonality in the *theta* between Smith and *Theodore*.

Figure 7 recapitulates the samples of the letters *theta*, *lambda*, and *tau* from Smith's handwriting, from *Theodore*, from the known Mar Saba manuscripts discussed above (Sabas 452, 518, and 523), plus samples from four additional Mar Saba manuscripts of the eighteenth century (Sabas 574, 591, 648, and 649). All three series of these letters are anomalous when compared with authentic Mar Saba manuscripts—all three resemble Smith's handwriting.

The manuscript is not what it appears to be. Instead of being scribed by an eighteenth-century monk at Mar Saba, the evidence shows that it was penned by an imitator whom Smith identified with a pseudonym that means "baldy" or "swindler," and a description that uncannily resembles Smith himself. Moreover, Smith's own handwriting exhibits several of the idiosyncrasies of the scribe of the *Secret Mark* manuscript, and therefore confirms the veracity of Smith's concealed claim of credit.

Smith's clues to the true nature of *Secret Mark* do not end with the manuscript, however. They are also embedded in the text of the letter *Theodore* and in *Secret Mark* itself.

4

The Modernity of *Theodore*

The letter to *Theodore* is a critical link in establishing the existence of *Secret Mark* in antiquity since there is no other evidence for *Secret Mark*'s existence independent of the Mar Saba manuscript. If Clement did in fact write *Theodore*, there seems little reason to doubt the existence of a text around A.D. 200 that Clement thought was a secret gospel of Mark. On the other hand, if Clement did not write *Theodore*, *Secret Mark*'s existence could be no more than a fiction of *Theodore*'s true author. Nevertheless, many scholars have been sufficiently impressed by Smith's case that the letter is genuinely Clementine that they have been willing to adopt the antiquity of *Secret Mark* as a "working hypothesis"—subject to a future, independent analysis of the manuscript.[1]

In our modern era of scholarship, deference to specialists is not only inevitable, but appropriate. Yet, the judgment of Clementine scholars has been more tentative than what some New Testament critics have expressed. For example, some biblical scholars point to the inclusion of *Theodore* in a revision of the standard critical edition for Clement as evidence that *Theodore* has been widely accepted as authentic,[2] but the editor of the revision merely printed *Theodore* provisionally ("provisorisch abdrucken")[3] for furthering discussion. Smith concurred with this status in 1982: "the recent 'provisional' inclusion of the letter in the Berlin edition of Clement's works adequately indicates its actual status."[4] Even this provisional status was rejected by a leading patristic specialist. Eric Osborn in his survey of a quarter-century of Clementine developments accorded "very little" probability for *Theodore* being genuine.[5] As a result, guarded statements such as "[i]f one accepts the authenticity of the fragmentary letter of Clement to Theodorus," remain a staple of Clementine scholarship today.[6]

Since scholarship remains divided, any assessment of the antiquity of *Secret Mark* should also include an assessment of *Theodore*. As Smith had recognized, "the supposition of forgery must be justified by demonstration either that the style or content of the work contains elements not likely to have come from the alleged author, or that some known historical circumstances would have furnished a likely occasion for the forgery" (*Clement* 89, n. 1). When Smith's own standards are applied to the *Theodore*, it is found that the supposition of fakery can be justified for at least the following reasons. The style of *Theodore* contains elements not likely to have come from Clement; in fact, it is hyper-Clementine, exaggerating certain of Clement's stylistic features while ignoring others. The content of *Theodore* contains elements not likely to have come from Clement, a letter from Clement, or from any period in Clement's life. Finally, *Theodore* contains elements that not only belong to the mid-twentieth century but also constitute clues to the identity of *Theodore*'s true author.

Theodore is Too Clementine to be True

It is clear that whoever wrote *Theodore* must have been familiar with Clement's extant writings because the number of *hapax legomena* in *Theodore*—i.e., vocabulary words found only in *Theodore* but not anywhere else in the previously recognized works of Clement—is very low. According to Smith's count, there are only seven such *hapax legomena* in *Theodore* out of a total vocabulary of 258 (*Clement* 67). A fundamental premise of stylistics is that an author's vocabulary is reasonably consistent among different works after taking into account differences in their genre and the author's age when they were written.[7] When applied to *hapax legomena*, as Smith did, the standard assumption is that the presence of too many words in a questioned work that are not found in the author's recognized vocabulary implies that the new work was not composed by that author. To put the statistic of seven *hapax legomena* into perspective, Smith compared *Theodore* with the works of Athanasius, finding 28 words unattested in Athananius's vocabulary (67). Smith's analysis thus ruled out Athanasius as the author of *Theodore*, and, based on this comparison as well as his similar analysis of the *Theodore* text at the phrasal, syntactical, and metrical levels, Smith concluded that "the letter is *either* entirely genuine *or* a deliberate imitation of Clement's style" (76, emphases original).

The major shortcoming of Smith's analysis, however, is that Smith did not look at the other end of an author's range of vocabulary usage, i.e., whether the number of *hapax legomena* in *Theodore* is too low as compared with the recognized writings of Clement. This deficiency was addressed in a study by Andrew Criddle, who analyzed *Theodore* using results from quantitative linguistic research that held that the percentage of *hapax legomena* in an author's body of work is relatively stable, decreasing only slightly with increase in the total size of the author's vocabulary.[8] For Clement of Alexandria, Criddle calculated this number to be about three-eighths (37.5 percent).[9] The relative stability of this percentage not only allows one to estimate whether the number of *hapax legomena* in a newly discovered work is too high, but also if the number is too low. In other words, when a new sample of the author's writing is found that introduces a new vocabulary word for that author, it should also contain approximately the right amount of words previously known to be *hapax legomena* so as to maintain that percentage. Criddle calculated that "for every increase in total vocabulary of eight in a new work or fragment of a previously unknown work by Clement one would estimate five words used only once in this previous work to occur again in the new work."[10] In other words, as eight new *hapax legomena* are found in a new sample of Clement's writing, five old *hapax legomena* should be eliminated, and the total number of *hapax legomena* in Clement's entire corpus should grow with each new discovery.

According to Smith's count, *Theodore* introduced seven new *hapax legomena*. If the percentage of Clement's *hapax legomena* is to be kept relatively stable, it is expected that *Theodore* should have used four or five vocabulary words previously thought to be *hapax legomena*. *Theodore* did not use four or five of these words but fifteen (*Clement* 68–69), for a net loss of seven *hapax legomena*.[11] In other words, instead of increasing the net total number of *hapax legomena* in Clement's writings by three for every eight completely new *hapax legomena* as expected, the Mar Saba letter attributed to Clement actually decreased the total by eight. Smith's unusual criteria for identifying *hapax legomena* may have skewed these figures, so Criddle applied more standard criteria and determined that *Theodore* actually introduced four new *hapax legomena* and eliminated nine previous *hapax legomena*.[12] Though not so extremely low as Smith's own count, the application of the standard criteria still entails a net loss of five *hapax legomena* rather than the expected increase. This discrepancy is so enormous that, despite the small size of the sample, it is statistically significant within the 2.5 percent level according to Criddle's calculations, well within the standard 5 percent level.[13]

Criddle's finding of a hyper-Clementine style in *Theodore* is not limited to vocabulary statistics of rare words. Similar problems exist in *Theodore*'s use of prepositions and his biblical citations. More than two thirds of the biblical passages that Clement quotes in his writings known before 1958 are only quoted once, but in *Theodore* only half of the eight biblical quotations are new with the other half having already been quoted in his recognized works. Based on this analysis, Criddle concluded that *Theodore* "contains too high a ratio of Clementine to non-Clementine traits to be authentic and should be regarded as a deliberate imitation of Clement's style."[14]

The excessively Clementine nature of *Theodore* is especially troubling because an author's vocabulary is only assumed to be reasonably stable in comparing two works of similar genre written by the author around the same age. This assumption is not applicable for *Theodore* because it is a letter not a philosophical treatise such as the *Stromateis*, which provides the bulk of Clement's extant vocabulary, nor a homily like *Quis dives salvatur*. If anything, *Theodore* should be less Clementine than his surviving works, but *Theodore* is not only more Clementine than expected, but excessively so.[15]

Criddle's findings are also important because they narrow the time-frame for the production of such a hyper-Clementine imitation. The meagerness of the manuscript tradition for Clement (*Clement* 286) would have made it a logistical nightmare, before the age of printing, to gather all of the works of Clement that survived long enough to be included in Stählin's concordance that Smith used to authenticate the letter. Since no manuscripts of Clement have survived at Mar Saba until the time of their transfer to Jerusalem,[16] it is unlikely that the imitator was isolated in Mar Saba. The imitator probably did not have access to the various lost works of Clement,[17] because the use of rare words from the lost works would have increased the extremely low number of *hapax legomena* in *Theodore* as compared with Clement's surviving works. This is another indication that the imitator's acquaintance with Clement's body of work is coextensive with the printed corpus of Clement's writings.

The imitation is probably even more recent than the dawn of printing.[18] The excessive avoidance of new *hapax legomena* for Clement belies an anxiety about passing modern tests of authenticity, which had begun emphasizing *hapax legomena* since the early 1800s.[19] The extent of the avoidance of *hapax legomena* in *Theodore* further suggests that such an imitation would have been impractical without the benefit of a concordance to Clement's writings, a task more arduous than composing a letter the length of *Theodore*. Quesnell observed that a close imitation of Clement was feasible after the publication of Stählin's index of Clement's vocabulary in 1936, to which Smith agreed.[20] Thus, the over-concentration of Clement's vocabulary and other stylistic features in *Theodore* is a justifiable reason to suspect that it is a deliberate imitation of Clement, one which was most practically executed some time after 1936.[21]

Theodore *is not a Personal Letter from Clement's Lifetime*

The next person after Quesnell to question the authenticity of *Secret Mark* seriously was Charles E. Murgia, who compared the text of *Theodore* with known classical fakes and found that it fit the profile of a forgery, especially in the use of a literary *sphragis*, or "seal of authenticity."[22] A literary *sphragis* is a textual device that authors sometimes use to identify themselves, usually by reminding their readers of their previous works.[23] The use of a literary *sphragis* to provide an internal warrant for a fake is particularly tempting to its creator because by its very nature the fake generally lacks the external evidence to corroborate its authenticity.[24] According to Murgia, *Theodore* has its *sphragis* immediately after the first line by alluding to Clement's condemnation of the Carpocratians already known to modern critics in his *Stromateis*.[25] In fact, Murgia concluded that "every sentence of the letter, other than the actual quotation of secret Mark, is admirably designed to provide a SEAL OF AUTHENTICITY for the passage of secret Mark."[26]

In his ten-year review of the critical response to *Secret Mark*, Smith seemed impressed by Murgia's analysis and responded to it as follows:

> Murgia, though he fell into a few factual errors, argued brilliantly that the literary form of the new document is one

found often in forgeries—a bogus introductory document, commonly a letter, explaining the appearance and vouching for the authenticity of the equally bogus material it presents. This is true, but the same form is often used for the presentation of genuine discoveries or material hitherto secret. Forgers use it because it is regularly used. (So too, when they forge wills, they commonly use the standard legal forms, but this does not prove that any will in a standard legal form is a forgery.) In sum, stimulating, but inconclusive. The question has to be settled by the objective evidence, above all the details of literary style. None of the studies contained any substantial argument to show that Clement could *not* have written the letter; they merely suggested reasons for thinking that someone else *might* have written it.[27]

Smith's counterargument does not work, even apart from Criddle's later demonstration that the letter was unlikely to have been written by Clement on stylistic grounds. Smith merely focused on *Theodore*'s vouching for *Secret Mark*, not on *Theodore*'s vouching for its own authenticity through the *sphragis* that Murgia identified at its very beginning. The importance of Murgia's observation is that a textual *sphragis* is an inappropriate security mechanism for the kind of letter that *Theodore* is. Private individuals in antiquity usually sent their letters by asking passing travelers to carry their letters, and, to ensure a minimal level of privacy, clay seals were often used.[28] If the letter's contents had to be more confidential, a trusted courier would be asked to deliver the letter personally.[29] Unless the sender is contemplating some eventual publication of the letter, it is unnecessary to use a *sphragis* to remind the reader who the writer is.

Unlike its genuine counterpart, a fictitious personal letter has to satisfy two, often incompatible, constraints to be plausible: it must appear as a believable personal letter to a purported addressee while simultaneously speaking to its external reader.[30] The tension between these goals imparts a kind of split personality to the letter, in which the voice of the purported writer sometimes has to break character to say something to the actual reader. As Patricia A. Rosenmeyer put it in her study of fictional letters in antiquity: "The communication of information unnecessary for the comprehension of the purported addressee, but critical for the appreciation of the external reader, is a frequent reminder of the fictionality of pseudonymous letters."[31] This is evident in *Theodore's* use of the *sphragis*.

Given the sensitive nature of the information contained in *Theodore*, an early third-century letter writer would have preferred delivery by a trusted courier. Thus, the *sphragis* of *Theodore* reminding the recipient of Clement's previous condemnation of the Carpocratians is gratuitous in its early third-century context. If *Theodore* was a private letter, Clement would have sent it by courier and, thus, its receiver would have been able to trust that Clement was the author without the *sphragis*. The private nature of *Theodore's* contents militates against Clement's contemplation of eventually publishing it. Thus, again, he would have felt no need to include the *sphragis*. In a modern imitation, however, it is vital in authenticating its author as Clement.

Rosenmeyer also identified the use of unnecessary clarifying details as a sign of "the public nature of the literary letter, written with posterity in mind."[32] In *Theodore*, such a detail is the specification that the secret gospel was still being kept "in Alexandria" (II.1). If Clement was still in Alexandria, the detail "in Alexandria" is unnecessary and "here" would have sufficed. Sensing this problem, Smith suggested that *Theodore* was written after he left Alexandria (*Clement* 48). But Attila Jakab found that this explanation raises more questions than answers. For example, it is puzzling why Theodore would write to Clement about a secret gospel kept in Alexandria if Clement had left Alexandria. Wouldn't Theodore have written to someone else, such as Origen, who was still there and presumably with access to the text?[33]

The problems of *Theodore* as an authentic personal letter do not end here. There are many other features that are more effective if it had a twentieth-century audience rather than if it were the third-century Theodore. For example, if Theodore had trusted what Clement would tell him about the secret gospel, then he would have been content with a simple denial from Clement that *Secret Mark* did not contain the troublesome text, "naked man with naked man." Quoting an entire passage from *Secret Mark*, which Theodore cannot independently check for accuracy, is unnecessary for him—but essential for modern scholars—to analyze its text.

The extensive quotation from *Secret Mark* raises another difficulty. Clement's quotations of gospel materials are usually so free that it is sometimes difficult to tell whether Clement used a different form of the text than what we now possess, or whether Clement was in the habit of quoting loosely and harmonizing to the other gospels and even to extra-canonical material.[34] By contrast, the Markan features in the *Secret Mark* passages are so salient that Clement must have quoted from it more meticulously than usual. Since Clement's decision to quote *Secret Mark* in the first place is unnecessary, Clement's unusual care in doing so is inexplicable. Moreover, for Clement to have quoted *Secret Mark* so carefully, he must have taken a copy of it with him—but this contradicts his own statement that it was guarded carefully in Alexandria.[35] On the other hand, *Theodore's* care in quoting the exact text of *Secret Mark*, even to the point of preserving its Semitisms (*Clement* 133–34), is vital for modern form critics to date the content to be earlier than the gospel of John.

There are other baffling aspects of the presumed setting. Why would Clement tell Theodore precisely where in the text of *Secret Mark* the nocturnal initiation story is located? Theodore's worry was ostensibly about whether the text contained "naked man with naked man" in support of the supposed homoeroticism of the Carpocratians.[36] The knowledge of where this passage belongs is immaterial to such concerns, but this information is extremely useful for modern source critics because it creates a literary sequence of passages that would imply a source document underlying *Secret Mark* and John, a source Smith did not fail to hypothesize (e.g. *Clement* 194).[37] Also useful to modern critics is the location of the *Secret Mark* pericope in chapter 10 of Mark, which is the only chapter of the gospels that Clement extensively quoted in his surviving works.[38]

There is another respect in which the third-century Clement inexplicably shares the same sensibilities and interests of a twentieth-century source critic: *Theodore* discloses far more details about the literary origin of the gospel of Mark than is typical for Clement's time. In particular, *Theodore* explicitly informs its recipient that Mark took notes, published a gospel from these notes, and then supplemented the public gospel with not only his notes but with Peter's notes. This kind of information comfortably fits into modernity's proclivity for dissecting texts into their sources but is very different from the usual, early Christian etiologies for Mark, which are tantalizingly brief and usually stress the role of Mark's memory.[39] In fact, it even differs from Clement's own explanation for the origin of Mark in his *Hypotyposeis*, "those present, who were many, entreated Mark, as one who followed him for a long time and remembered what was said, to record what was spoken," an explanation that also emphasizes Mark's memory, not his note-taking ability.[40]

The Anachronisms of Theodore *Identify its Author*

Smith's main argument in favor of attributing *Theodore* to Clement is that no person so intimately familiar with Clement's works as to produce such a fine imitation of his style would have tolerated the blatant contradictions between *Theodore* and the recognized body of Clement's work (*Clement* 84–85).[41] In particular, Smith noted that the letter contradicts Clement's attested views on swearing oaths and attributes the founder of the Carpocratians to Carpocrates himself instead of his son Epiphanes. Despite these obvious problems, Smith argued that these contradictions were only apparent and could be reconciled with the "private character and stated purpose" of *Theodore* that could well include "material at which his published works would barely hint" (*Clement* 83, 85).[42] Smith's argument implies that the authenticity of *Theodore* would be vulnerable to a contradiction with Clement's recognized works that could not be explained by any private purpose for *Theodore*. If such a contradiction can be found, Smith's carefully crafted argument that *Theodore* is not an expert imitation falls apart.

One such contradiction lies in the interpretation of *Theodore* and the application of Jesus' saying at Matthew 5:13 and Luke 14:34 about salt losing its flavor. In the letter, the salt saying is applied as follows: "For the true things being mixed with inventions, are falsified, so that, as the saying goes, even the salt loses its savor" (*Theod.* I.13–15). The letter's interpretation is premised on an image of mixing table salt with an adulterant that changes its flavor. *Theodore*'s explanation is immediately problematic for Clementine authorship because it contradicts a very different analogy employed by Clement for elucidating this difficult saying. In *Stromateis* 1.8.41.3–4, a passage Smith did not discuss in his treatment of this part of *Theodore* (*Clement* 18–19), Clement wrote:

> (3) "There are many people," he says, "who refuse to take instructions, talk nonsense and spread false ideas." So everyone was being addressed by the words "You are the salt of the earth." (4) Some of the hearers of the Word are like fish of the sea. They have grown up in saltwater from birth and even so need salt in their preparation.[43]

Clement noticed that some things can grow up in a salty environment but still not taste salty. Just as a fish taken out of salt water does not taste salty and still needs to be salted, so do people brought up in the teaching of the church lose their

saltiness when they are removed from it.[44] By contrast, the salt
saying as applied in *Theodore* does not connect the loss of salt's
flavor to the removal from an environment where the truth is
taught, but rather to the mixing of truth and error in such a
setting.

The interpretation of *Theodore* is therefore un-Clementine,
but there is a more serious problem: it presupposes salt-making
technology that did not exist in Clement's place and time. The
imagery in *Theodore* involves mixing an adulterant with salt
and spoiling its taste. For salt to be mixed with such an adulterant, it would have to be loose and free-flowing, but free-
flowing salt is a modern invention. Pure salt draws moisture
from the air, forming clumps, and often requires a mallet to be
broken apart for domestic use. In 1910, however, a chemist at
the Morton Salt Company discovered that salt's tendency to
form clumps in humidity can be prevented by adding a small
amount of an anti-caking agent to uniform-sized salt crystals
obtained from vacuum-pan evaporation. Morton Salt's technological advance and its famous advertising slogan, "When it
rains, it pours," enabled the company to monopolize the
American market for table salt throughout most of the twentieth century.[45]

Throughout much of history, salt has been distributed in
clumped forms such as blocks or lumps, and Clement's writings
describe salt as being in the form of lumps (e.g., ἁλῶν χόνδροι
in *Protr.* 2.14.2, 2.22.4, and *Strom.* 7.4.26). In fact, salt added
at the table was a minor source of dietary salt in antiquity
because prepared foodstuffs already had plenty of salt due to its
preservative properties. A good example is the salted fish
Clement used to analogize the salt saying in *Stromateis* 1.8.3–4.

The analysis of the salt saying in *Theodore* is also problematic
because it presumes that the letter's recipient would have
appreciated the adulteration of salt as a problem. Though adulteration of many other foodstuffs, usually by adding inexpensive ingredients to more expensive products, was certainly a

serious issue in Western antiquity, evidence of the adulteration of salt itself is lacking even in Pliny's encyclopedic discussion of adulterated foodstuffs.[46] Adulterating salt would have made little economic sense because salt was a commodity so inexpensive that monopolies of Egyptian salt guilds had to set and enforce minimum prices on salt sales by their members. For example, one guild ordinance from the first century C.E. set a fine for violating their price floor: "And if anyone shall sell at a lower price than these, let such a one be fined eight drachmas in silver for the common fund and the same for the public treasury."[47] Though the nonexistence of adulterated salt in the ancient sources is admittedly an argument from silence, the insignificance of adulterated salt to Pliny in his otherwise enxtensive treatment means that *Theodore*'s allusion would have been ineffective for its purported era.

To the modern reader of *Theodore*, on the other hand, the salt allusion is natural: free-flowing salt was and continues to be mixed with other ingredients perceived as affecting its taste. This was particularly true starting in the 1930s when Morton Salt added another ingredient to their table salt, harsh-tasting potassium iodide for the prevention of endemic goiter.[48] *Theodore*'s salt imagery, so readily comprehensible to Smith's contemporaries, is an anachronism that reveals it to be a modern invention. Many fakes have been exposed because they contained materials that were not technologically produced at the time of their supposed origin. For example, an illuminated manuscript known as Archaic Mark, now housed at the University of Chicago, was found to contain the pigment Prussian Blue, which was not produced before 1704.[49] The technological anachronism of *Theodore* is no less damning.

This anachronism involves the kind of minor detail that may well have easily been overlooked by its twentieth-century creator, but it is more likely a deliberately embedded clue. Morton Smith, the putative discoverer of *Theodore*, shares his given name with Morton Salt the company that invented the type of salt *Theodore* evokes. But the clues do not stop there. More are found in his commentary about this passage in *Theodore*. In fact, Smith considered this passage to be highly probative of the genuineness of *Theodore*:

> Behind the choice of this proverb probably lies not only recollection of the context of these Gospel passages (and Mk. 9.50), which declare corrupted Christians fit only to be cast out, but also the recollection of Jeremiah 28.17 (LXX) (= 10.14 Heb.) ἐμωράνθη πᾶς ἄνθρπος ἀπὸ γνώσεως . . . ὅτι ψευδῆ ἐχώνευσαν, οὐκ ἔστιν πνεῦμα ἐν αὐτοῖς (and ff.), which made the verse particularly appropriate for use against gnostics who had corrupted the Scriptures. This sort of multiple biblical allusion is typical of Clement and would be very difficult for a forger to imitate. (*Clement* 18–19)

The inventiveness of the allusion to the Jeremiah text, however, is due more to Smith than to Clement. The verse quoted from Jeremiah means "every person is made dull from knowledge . . . because they have cast false things, there is no breath in them,"[50] but the linkage to Matthew 5:13's use of "cast out" works only in English, not in Greek. The Greek word for "cast out" at Matthew 5:13 is βληθὲν ἔξω, which means "to throw outside," but the verb in Jeremiah, ἐχώνευσαν, refers to shaping metal objects by melting and pouring into a mold. Indeed, the Jeremiah passage has nothing to do with salt or mixing truth and lies but clearly refers to the creation of a false thing. The only verbal commonality in the Greek lies in different forms of the verb μωρανθῆναι/ἐμωράνθη ("to be silly, foolish" or "to make tasteless"). Such an allusion based on casting out could only be "typical of Clement" if Clement knew English.

Smith's attempt to create an allusion to Jeremiah 28:17 is so fallacious in light of his otherwise superlative exegetical ability that another explanation for his analysis must be sought. Smith's next sentence in his commentary is an important clue: "In III.183.23ff. Clement identifies as 'the salt of the earth' those 'more elect than the elect,' 'who hide away, in the depth of thought, the mysteries not to be uttered'" (*Clement* 19). The connection between Morton Smith and Morton Salt signifies that this comment applies to himself—that he has hidden away a mystery not to be uttered. Smith's use of an ellipsis in the Jeremiah 28:17 passage is the "unuttered mystery" to which he then refers. The unuttered text within the ellipses reads: κατησχύνθη πᾶς χρυσοχόος ἀπὸ τῶν γλυπτῶν αὐτοῦ ("every goldsmith is confounded because of his graven images").[51] Taking Smith at his word that "the verse [is] particularly appropriate for use against gnostics who had corrupted the Scriptures," *Secret Mark* is not just a corruption of the gospel of Mark but a graven image that will confound its own smith: Morton Smith.

There are thus two clues to *Theodore*'s creator: a reference to a Morton embedded in the text and another to a Smith buried in the commentary for that text. Either clue is clever by itself—but their combination is ingenious. These clues identify both the given name and the surname of a person, but not just any person, the one who found himself at Mar Saba staring at its text. What we have is the hoaxer's second confession.

If this is a confession, is it credible? Quesnell argued that it was possible to imitate Clement of Alexandria using Stählin's concordance and Smith agreed. Speculating on a potential imitator, Smith stated: "Perhaps, with Stählin's index to Clement and recent stylistic studies, he could also compose three pages in Clement's style. Perhaps, if he had worked on Clement for years, he might even catch Clement's habits of thought and forms of exposition."[52] Nevertheless, Smith characterized his familiarity with Clement as follows: "I have never published an article on Clement nor even reviewed a book on him."[53] Smith's denial, though technically accurate as an issue of bibliography, did not quite address the level of experience that Smith just agreed was necessary—and Smith had that level of experience. His "Image of God" article published just a few months before his return to Mar Saba demonstrates his own facility with Clement of Alexandria. He cited Clement four times, once explicitly identifying his familiarity with Stählin's edition.[54] As previously noted, Smith personally owned a copy of Stählin's critical edition of Clement. Smith's second confession, too, is credible.

5

The Modernity of *Secret Mark*

Most scholars agree that *Secret Mark* postdates the canonical Mark.[1] The only evidence for the existence of *Secret Mark* in antiquity is a single copy of a letter purportedly by Clement of Alexandria. Both the manuscript and the content of the letter have now been shown to be twentieth-century productions attributed to Morton Smith. Since there is no other evidence for the antiquity of *Secret Mark*, it is reasonable to question the *Secret Mark*'s antiquity as well. But the case for reattributing *Secret Mark* to Morton Smith is stronger than showing that it has been misattributed; it also rests on evidence that it itself belongs to the twentieth century and owes its origin to Morton Smith.

Secret Mark *Belongs to the Twentieth Century*

In a recent treatment of *Secret Mark*, Bart Ehrman began on the right track with the following questions:

> [O]ne does need to take into account some of the peculiar details. Why would the text stress that this fellow was completely naked under his linen garment and that Jesus spent the night with him? . . . Rather than pursue that question, I want to deal with the prior one. Is this an authentic letter of Clement, or was it forged? And if it was forged, forged by whom?[2]

Though Ehrman went on to discuss the issue of forgery without coming to a "definitive answer," it turns out that Ehrman's
first question contains the key to answering his other questions. The climax of *Secret Mark* occurs in an intriguing sentence at *Theodore* III.8–10: καὶ ἔμεινε σὺν αὐτῷ τὴν νύκτα
ἐκείνην ἐδίδασκεν γὰρ αὐτόν ὁ᾽ Ἰησοῦς τὸ μυστήριον τῆς βασι-
λείας τοῦ Θεοῦ ("And he remained with him that night for
Jesus taught him the mystery of the kingdom of God"). The
latter part of this sentence is a close parallel to Mark 4:11 but
the main clause does not parallel the gospels but rather is
crafted by the author of *Secret Mark*.[3] Both its climactic location and its composed, unparalleled nature indicate that it was
carefully constructed by its author.

Yet the compositional importance of the sentence does not
match its meaning. Taken literally, the sentence states that he
spent that night with him, but the *Secret Mark* passage had
already presented Jesus as visiting at the young man's home
(*Theod.* III.6, ἦλθον εἰς τὴν οἰκίαν τοῦ νεανίσκου). The clause's
bland recital of their lodging arrangement thus conveys almost
no additional information and belongs more to the background, for instance, with something like: "Jesus taught him
the mystery of the kingdom of God, for he spent that night
with him." Unless the clause has an idiomatic meaning that
goes beyond mere lodging, it is difficult to account for the compositional importance of this clause in the *Secret Mark* passage.
With regard to the meaning of this clause, Smith stated that
Secret Mark "probably derived its phrase from common usage,
not from a literary source" (*Clement* 117), but his otherwise
detailed commentary failed to cite any Greek text with a clause
that would show the phrase's meaning or frequency. In Smith's
day, the claim that a phrase is in "common usage" can be difficult to verify, since concordances existed for only a small portion of Greek literature. Today is different, however, because
the *Thesaurus Linguae Graecae* (TLG) project has amassed a
digital database of ancient and medieval Greek texts compris-

ing about 91,000,000 words distributed among approximately 3,700 authors and 12,000 works. A search of the online TLG database with the most recent update of April 29, 2005, for clauses containing a form of μένω, the preposition σύν, and the accusative νύκτα has failed to turn up a single instance of that phrase outside of this text.[4]

Another oddity about the clause is Smith's wooden translation of it into English, despite his repeated advocacy for idiomatic renderings.[5] A more natural rendering in English is "and he spent that night with him" as some scholars have adopted in recent translations.[6] But in the mid-twentieth century, Smith had good reason to avoid that rendering because it would have been too sexually charged in American English as a euphemism for casual sex. R. W. Holder's *Dictionary of Euphemisms* defines the phrase *spend the night with* as "to copulate with casually. Of either sex usually in a transient relationship," and cites an example by Louis Armstrong dating to 1955.[7] By 1965, the euphemistic meaning of *spend the night* was so entrenched that a popular writer's handbook gave it as an example when euphemism should be used: "It may be preferable to write that a man and woman 'spent the night together' than to go into detail just how they spent it."[8] For *Secret Mark*, this sexually charged meaning was explicitly recognized by at least one contemporary, Smith himself:

> Since the Carpocratians had a reputation for sexual license (see Appendix B) and this section of the longer text reported that a youth came to Jesus περιβεβλημένος σινδόνα ἐπὶ γυμνοῦ and stayed with him all night, it is easy to suppose that the Carpocratians took the opportunity to insert in the text some material which would authorize the homosexual relationship Clement suggested by picking out γυμνὸς γυμνῷ. (*Clement* 185)[9]

To a twentieth-century scholar, the main *Secret Mark* passage culminates with a euphemistic suggestion of a casual sexual encounter between the young man and Jesus. Euphemism "is the language of evasion, of hypocrisy, of prudery, and of deceit" by providing deniability to its speaker because "the euphemistic word or phrase once meant, or prima facie still means, something else."[10] This aspect is also true of "spend the night with someone." The *Bloomsbury Dictionary of Euphemisms* regards the phrase as "an even more coy circumlocution than sleep with: we are invited to consider the possibility of the two people sitting up until dawn discussing Chinese philosophy or the current economic crisis."[11] In *Secret Mark*, they are discussing the mystery of the kingdom of God.

The intrinsic evasiveness of euphemisms means that their innuendo runs the risk of being missed unless it is reinforced. Significantly, *Secret Mark* contains several features that not only reinforce the sexual meaning for twentieth-century readers but also block that interpretation for second-century readers. For example, *Secret Mark* contains explicit statements of love between the two males plus Jesus' rejection of three different women.[12] These details are critical for the twentieth-century reader in assigning a sexual identity to Jesus in terms of an exclusive sexual preference that supports the sexual import of his spending the night with a man.[13]

On the other hand, these details would have been lost on an ancient reader of *Secret Mark*. While the scholarly debate continues between the "essentialist" camp and the "social construction" camp over whether people in antiquity were homosexual in the modern sense, there is broader agreement, however, that sexual orientation was not used to define sexual identity in Greek antiquity.[14] Because of *Secret Mark*'s presentation of Jesus and the young man as social peers, none of the professions of love between Jesus and the young man nor Jesus' rejection of three women within *Secret Mark* would have defined Jesus' sexual identity to an ancient reader as easily as it would define it for the modern reader.

In antiquity, societal position was crucial. Same-sex relationships between males were conventionally depicted between people of unequal social stations, for instance, between an adult male and a boy (παῖς), or between a male citizen and a slave. Same-sex acts between male citizens, on the other hand, were problematic because one of them would have had to behave inconsistently with his social position.[15] A story in the Hellenistic novel under the name of Xenophon of Ephesus is instructive (*Ephesiaca* 3.2). The novel describes a same-sex affair between a young man Hippothous (νέος) and a teen Hyperanthes (μειράκοιν). While their relationship remained socially unequal with Hippothous as the dominant partner, their closeness in age made their relationship undetectable.[16]

Secret Mark presents the two men as social peers. The young man was a wealthy property owner ("the house of the youth, for he was rich") and Jesus was a messianic claimant ("Son of David"). In terms of age, however, the "young man" of *Secret Mark* is not the παῖς in conventional depictions, nor even the teen of *Ephesiaca* 3.2, but the older νεανίσκος. Descriptions of a νεανίσκος or νέος ("young man") place the beginning of this age at around twenty-one years (e.g., Diogenes Laertius, *Vit.* 8.10; Philo, *Opif.* 105).[17] *Secret Mark's* presentation of them as peers hinders the ancient reader from identifying the sexually charged significance that the phrase *spending the night with him* makes so obvious to the modern reader. On the other hand, relationships between social peers are common today among same-sex couples, and the social equality of the young man and Jesus reinforces for modern readers the sexual innuendo of *Secret Mark* that was blocked to ancient readers.

Few social constructions are so well defined as the legal system and *Secret Mark* even contains a datable reference to modern law enforcement activities against urban gay men. The recent Supreme Court decision legalizing private, consensual homosexual activity based its decision on the evolution of legal attitudes against such behavior over the course of history, especially during the twentieth century.[18] The Court's observation agrees with modern research that the 1950s were "an especially oppressive period for homosexual men in America,"[19] and many American cities in the 1950s intensified enforcement of municipal disorderly conduct offences to arrest gay men for seeking each other in public parks.[20] In New York City, for instance, the relevant ordinance applied to any person who "frequents or loiters about any public place soliciting men for the purpose of committing a crime against nature or other lewdness."[21] This ordinance was in effect from its enactment in 1923 until it was ruled unconstitutional in 1983.[22]

The description in *Secret Mark* of the young man's clothing ("wearing a linen cloth over his naked body") uses the same language found in Mark 14:51-52 to describe the youth who fled from Gethsemane when Jesus was arrested, a textual link that implies that both young men came to Jesus seeking the same thing (an inference Smith drew in *Clement* 177; *Secret Gospel* 81). The sexually charged climax of *Secret Mark* means that what these young men were seeking was, to use the words of the New York statute, "a crime against nature or other lewdness." In other words, *Secret Mark* easily conjures up to the twentieth-century reader the image that Jesus was arrested for soliciting a homoerotic encounter in a public garden. An ancient reader of *Secret Mark*, on the other hand, would not have recognized the public solicitation offence because it did not exist in Clement's day. Indeed, jurists contemporary to Clement were only just beginning to expand the crime of *stuprum* in the *Lex Julia de adulteriis* to encompass homosexual acts with minors. Male prostitution continued to be tolerated until Emperor Philip (died A.D. 249),[23] but neither extension of the law is implicated in *Secret Mark*. Not even Jeremy Bentham writing in 1817, who calls the youth of Mark 14:51-52 a "loosely attired stripling" and identified him as a "cinaedus," made such a connection between Jesus' arrest in the garden and homoeroticism.[24] *Secret Mark*'s linkage between its sexually charged nocturnal initiation and Jesus' arrest in the garden resonates only within a specific moment within a changing twentieth-century legal landscape that peaked in the 1950s. That *Secret Mark* came to light in 1958 is no coincidence.

Thus *Secret Mark* works very differently in the twentieth century in which it was found than in the first or second century in which it is supposed to have been written. To readers of the 1950s, *Secret Mark* builds up to a climax that employs a recent euphemism describing a homoerotic encounter between Jesus and a young man—a description reinforced by information about their sexual orientation, age, social locations, and arrest in the garden of Gethsemane. It was scandalous for its day. To ancient readers, however, the text anticlimaxed in a banality about where they lodged that night. The uncanny resonance of *Secret Mark* with mid-twentieth-century notions of sexual identity and legal regimes is no less a telling anachronism than *Theodore*'s reference to the mid-twentieth-century iodization of table salt and the manuscript's modern letter forms.

Secret Mark's Seal of Authorship Identifies its Author

The sexual innuendo that made *Secret Mark* such an interesting and potentially momentous find is now part of what identifies it as a modern fake, but it also does more than that—it is also Morton Smith's own *sphragis* that declares his authorship by alluding to his previous works. The climax of the nocturnal initiation of *Secret Mark* contains a juxtaposition of Mark 4:11 and a sexual practice forbidden in Jewish law (Lev 18:22, 20:13) and is embedded in a letter by Clement of Alexandria exhorting secrecy. These elements had already been connected to each other in Smith's publications before the summer of 1958. For example, in his dissertation, *Tannaitic Parallels to the Gospels*, published in 1951, Smith associated Mark 4:11 with secrecy over forbidden sexual relationships:

> Further I think the passage in Sifre on Deut. to have been based on the fact that an important part of primitive Christianity was a secret doctrine which was revealed only

to trusted members. Such a doctrine is suggested by the words put in the mouth of Jesus, speaking to his disciples: 'To you is given the mystery of the kingdom of God, but to those outside all things are in parables, that they may surely see and not perceive.' etc. And Paul himself wrote in I Cor. 2.1-6. . . .[25] A similar distinction was recognized by the Tannaïm between material suitable for public teaching and that reserved for secret teaching, as we learn from Hagigah T 2.1 (233): 'The (passages of the Old Testament dealing with) forbidden sexual relationships are not to be expounded to three (at a time), . . .'[26]

If Smith's linkage of Mark 4:11 with forbidden sexual relationships in *T. Hag.* 2.1 in 1951 and *Secret Mark*'s coupling of Mark 4:11 with a forbidden sexual relationship are to be considered merely a lucky coincidence, Smith's prior knowledge of linking Clement of Alexandria to these passages would be harder to explain away, since Smith barely mentioned Clement before 1958. However, in an article published in March of 1958, Smith revisited this Talmudic passage right before he returned to Mar Saba:[27]

We should not expect this doctrine to be developed in the preserved rabbinic material, since the teaching of the throne of God is specified as that to be kept most secret of all,[4] and quite possibly was not committed to writing.[5]

[4] Hagigah 2.1 and parallels.
[5] Cf. Clement of Alexandria, *Strom.* 1.1.13-14 etc.

Coleman-Norton's possession of the subject matter of his text prior to his supposed discovery of it was conclusive for Metzger to recognize the "amusing *agraphon*" as a fake and Coleman-Norton as its faker. Likewise, Smith's possession of the crucial linkage between Mark's mystery of the kingdom of God, forbidden sexual practices, and Clement of Alexandria's discussion of secrecy is what authenticates his own claim of authorship to *Secret Mark* through the *sphragis* crafted in the climax.

6

Morton Smith's *Secret* Uncovered

Secret Mark is not what it appears to be. All three components of *Secret Mark*—the pseudo-Markan fragments of a secret gospel, the letter ascribed to Clement of Alexandria, and the physical manuscript itself—are twentieth-century imitations. The manuscript was written in what may appear to be handwriting of the eighteenth century, but the hesitation and shakiness of its strokes and the retouching of its letters, coupled with twentieth-century letter forms, indicate that the handwriting is actually a drawn imitation of an eighteenth-century style. *Theodore*, too, is an impersonation, mimicking the style and vocabulary of Clement of Alexandria but contradicting him with a simile that evokes modern salt-making technology. *Secret Mark* is also an imitation, with its Markan parallels deviating only at its climax, in language that resonates with mid-twentieth-century expressions of sexuality. On three independent grounds and at three different levels, *Secret Mark* is a deliberate, but ultimately imperfect, imitation.

Even more conclusive than the evidence that *Secret Mark* is a modern fake is Smith's own triple confession to his involvement in all three components of *Secret Mark*. He gave a self-descriptive pseudonym of M. Madiotes for the scribe, he inserted allusions to his own name in *Theodore* and the accompanying commentary, and he put a *sphragis* to his own writings at the climax of the *Secret Mark* fragment. Though uncoerced confessions are among the most persuasive evidence in criminal trials, confessions are not necessarily truthful, and Smith's admissions must be analyzed critically. In the classic, analytical framework of the "means, motive, and opportunity" triad, Smith meets all three criteria and it is hard to identify anyone else as suitable as Smith.

Smith Had the Rare Combination of Abilities

Very few people had the means or ability to create all three components of the fake, and whoever did so ideally would have been familiar with the library at Mar Saba, eighteenth-century Greek handwriting, transmission of patristic letters, Stählin's edition of Clement of Alexandria, heresiology, and the gospel of Mark. Smith was proficient in all these areas, a remarkable feat considering the specialization of the discipline. While most of those questioning *Secret Mark* have shown a healthy respect for—if not dread of—his abilities, it has been only recently that a defender of *Secret Mark*'s antiquity has argued that Smith lacked the ability to do it.

In particular, Scott G. Brown contended: "Those most profi-cient in classical Greek tended to think that the letter sur-passed Smith's ability."[1] Brown did not cite a source for this anonymous disparagement, and, whoever these people are, their assessment must lack familiarity with Smith's scholarship, which as early as 1945 cogently critiqued some of Edgar Goodspeed's translations for missing nuances of the Greek original.[2] Furthermore, those who worked closely with Smith for years have noticed that Smith's language skills were excep-tional. For instance, Shaye J. D. Cohen wrote: "Smith was a man who worked comfortably in Greek, Latin, and Hebrew, and had a good working knowledge of Syriac."[3]

Perhaps Brown was thinking of Murgia's back-handed exon-eration of Smith, "his knowledge of Greek seems inferior to that of the author," but the reliability of Murgia's spoken remark must be questioned because Murgia was also unaware of Smith's sense of humor.[4] While the basis for Murgia's opinion of Smith's Greek is not entirely clear, it is not improbable that Murgia identified some of Smith's deliberate howlers—e.g., using an English-language pun to connect Matthew 5:13 and Jeremiah 28:17—yet failed to realize their significance.[5] Perhaps Brown's source is Smith's own self-deprecating remark that "nobody else has had so high an opinion of my classical scholarship."[6] Strictly speaking, Smith's remark is beside the point because Mark, Clement of Alexandria, and an eighteenth-century Sabaite monk all postdate the classical period. Smith's terminology of "classical scholarship" need not include Greek at all, and even if it did, it would not encompass the later Greek in which *Secret Mark* and *Theodore* were written. At any rate, Smith's invitation to Mar Saba to catalog Greek manuscripts is compelling evidence of Smith's high level of competence in Greek at least as far as the Greek Orthodox Patriarchate of Jerusalem was concerned.

Brown continued to be pessimistic about Smith's abilities. For example, Brown asserted that "Smith published nothing on Clement prior to the 1970s and showed little interest in patristics in the period leading up to his discovery."[7] Smith's bibliography says otherwise. It is incorrect that "Smith published nothing on Clement prior to the 1970s" as Brown claimed because Smith's "Image of God" article in March 1958 cited Clement of Alexandria four times.[8] As for Smith's interest in patristics, he published "The Manuscript Tradition of Isidore of Pelusium" in 1954, "An Unpublished Life of St. Isidore of Pelusium" in 1958, and "The Description of the Essenes in Josephus and the Philosophumena" in 1958.[9] Both Isidore of Pelusium and Hippolytus are patristic authors, and the two articles published in 1958 took years of research.[10] Another of Brown's doubts over Smith's abilities resembles a request for evidence:

The people who foster the romantic notion that Smith was capable of imitating the handwriting and aged appearance of an eighteenth-century manuscript have not produced any supporting evidence, let alone demonstrated that Smith had developed any expertise in Clement prior to 1958.[11]

Supporting evidence for these points can be found in, for example, Smith's 1956 article, "Σύμμεικτα." In that article, Smith discussed the fruits of his 1951–1952 visit to monasteries in Greece, which included dozens of manuscripts, many of them from the eighteenth century, even commenting on their inaccuracies in orthography and accentuation. Smith recorded that he had taken photographs of Dimitsane MS 22, a manuscript of over 150 pages and written in an eighteenth-century hand.[12] As for having "any expertise in Clement," Smith's March 1958 article, "Image of God," published just months before his second visit to Mar Saba demonstrates exactly such expertise.

Although full bibliographies for Smith now list more than 280 separate works, less than thirty were published by the summer of 1958.[13] In the bibliographies for Brown's dissertation and his book, none of the six articles discussed here that could have substantiated a more positive and realistic assessment of Smith's abilities were listed.[14]

Smith Had Just the Right Opportunity

Stroumsa's confirmation that the manuscript of *Secret Mark* was at Mar Saba in 1976 means that whoever faked the text needed the opportunity to introduce it into that isolated place. Because there is no evidence that the manuscript or the book had been present at Mar Saba prior to 1958, the window of opportunity included Smith's second visit to Mar Saba. The book's size meant it was easily concealed, and, whatever the security arrangements of the thirteen monks at Mar Saba were, it is doubtful that they included preventing a guest from smuggling a book *into* the monastery.

Even if there existed someone else as capable as Smith in the diverse set of fields necessary to produce the fake, that person must have had the opportunity to plant it at Mar Saba in time for Smith to discover it. But, to account for the parallels between Smith's article published in March of 1958 and his visit to Mar Saba just a few months later, the window of opportunity is minuscule—for anyone other than Smith—to compose the text based on painstaking research using Stählin, obtain an appropriate book to write it in, practice the Greek hand in such a short span of time, and obtain permission to visit Mar Saba right before Smith's visit.

Given the opportunity afforded by *Secret Mark*, Smith did not behave like the victim of a fake. *Secret Mark* did not become a major factor in his scholarship apart from the books disclosing it to the world. Smith's next major work, *Jesus the Magician*, though often citing the collection of background information published in *Clement*, was careful not to rely on *Secret Mark* itself. Indeed, Brown remarked that *Jesus the Magician* "could have been written without the discovery of the longer gospel,"[15] finding that *Secret Mark* was "discussed on only two pages of this book, 134–35, and is briefly mentioned in three endnotes on pp. 203, 207 and 210," identifying several places where Smith could have mentioned *Secret Mark* but failed to do so, and documenting that Smith's "basic neglect of longer Mark" continued in his later works.[16]

In fact, Brown was not the only one to notice Smith's non-use of *Secret Mark*. Another person was a reviewer who made the mistake of stating that Smith's *Jesus the Magician* depended on *Secret Mark*. Smith excoriated him as follows:

> I am sorry to have to ask you to print the following corrections of the false statements and insinuations made by F. Kermode in his review (*NYR*, October 26) of my book *Jesus the Magician* (Harper & Row, San Francisco, 1978). . . . In this argument, clearly, the fragment of secret Mark plays no substantial part. It contributes only one or two confirmatory

details to the mass of evidence. Kermode's statement that *Jesus the Magician* rests on the secret gospel fragment is utterly untrue.[17]

In other matters Smith did not behave like the innocent victim of a fake. Though challenged, Smith did not attempt to go back to Mar Saba to obtain additional physical evidence or even to publish non-cropped photographs of the text. In fact, his last will and testament ordered his correspondence in which he may have exposed his involvement to be destroyed.[18]

Smith Had the Motives

Turning to motive, an unfortunate aspect in the history of the discussion of *Secret Mark* has been the use of the term *forgery*. Although *Secret Mark* may literally meet the common definition of a literary forgery as "created or modified with the intention to deceive," forgery often connotes a narrower set of motives, namely, to defraud for obtaining money, property, or a legal right, or, in academic contexts, to fabricate evidence in favor of one's theories. Thus, forgery essentially connotes a crime of cheating. These connotations do not apply to *Secret Mark*. *Secret Mark* is not a legal instrument, such as a check, a will, or even the *Donation of Constantine*. Neither Smith nor anyone associated with Smith attempted to sell *Secret Mark* for money or other valuable consideration.

While the circumstances surrounding *Secret Mark* do not support the conclusion that it is a criminal forgery done to defraud, that does not exhaust the possibilities of its being a twentieth-century fake. *Secret Mark* could also be a *hoax*. Although hoaxes share with forgeries the element of creating a document with the intention to deceive, hoaxes are done with a different motive—to test the establishment, whether to expose flaws in the gatekeepers of authenticity, to exhibit one's skill and cunning, or to take pleasure in the failure of self-appointed experts to pass the test.

Secret Mark functions as a hoax designed to test, not a forgery designed to cheat. The intricate three-level textual puzzle of *Secret Mark* is a challenging test of its creator's mastery of a diversity of demanding fields and the academy's ability to authenticate. Further testing the academy, Smith planted various clues about *Secret Mark's* nature as a hoax in places scholars typically do not look. First, Smith published another sample of the same hand of *Theodore* in his popular treatment while attributing it to a twentieth-century individual with a pseudonym that means both "baldy" and "swindler" in his modern Greek catalog published in an obscure periodical. Second, the salt metaphor employed in *Theodore* that invokes the iodization of table salt by the Morton Salt Company is not only a subtle anachronism but also an allusion to its actual inventor. Third, the climax to *Secret Mark* functions as Smith's own literary seal. These clues are Smith's triune confession.

The jokes embedded in *Secret Mark* also identify the motive as hoaxing. As Harold Love has noted: "fakers rarely resist a concealed joke or two, just to rub home how supremely clever they are."[19] *Secret Mark* abounds in jokes, including the text's cliffhanger ending right before the passage was to be explained, the pop culture reference to an evangelical thriller, and the excessively suitable book it was written in. Smith's publications continued to drop hints that *Secret Mark* was a hoax, including his preface ("No doubt if the past, like a motion picture, could be replayed, I should also be shocked to find how much of the story I have already invented," *Secret Gospel* ix), and his conclusion that "truth is necessarily stranger than history" (*Secret Gospel* 148). Most of the attention, however, has been paid to Smith's intriguing dedication for his *Secret Gospel* ("to the one who knows"), because Smith dedicated *Clement* to Arthur Darby Nock, a skeptic of *Secret Mark*.[20] These jokes identify what kind of fake *Secret Mark* is.

The desire to prove himself makes sense for the particular moment in Smith's career. *Secret Mark* was composed at a vulnerable point in his life when few people of importance appreciated his abilities. He was denied tenure in 1955 at the university where he started his career. Smith was forty years old and might have been perceived as over-the-hill. A successful hoax could be exactly what Smith needed to prove to himself that he was smarter than his peers and might even jump start his career in the process.

But this motive can only be a partial explanation, at the very least because it was overtaken by events. Smith saved his career well before he published *Clement* and *Secret Gospel* in 1973. He landed a position at Columbia in 1957, authored a successful textbook in ancient history in 1960, and was made a full professor in 1962.[21] Even though he was unable to obtain an appointment to Harvard that he desired, he nonetheless had tenure at Columbia.[22] Yet Smith maintained the hoax.

Motives are rarely simple or pure, and motives that were auxiliary at the beginning can take on greater importance later. For scholarly fakes, Grafton has identified one motive that frequently accompanies ambition:

> Since forgeries are intellectual and scholarly projects, and often far from trivial ones, the invocation of motives and ambitions rarely explains them fully. Most forgeries of any scale and depth strive not only to advance the career of their creator but to support his beliefs and opinions.[23]

Before discussing how *Secret Mark* supports his opinions, one pitfall must be avoided. In previous discussions of Smith's motives, many people have been tempted to cite the ideas contained in Smith's two books describing *Secret Mark*. Those are probably the worst places to look for the beliefs and opinions that *Secret Mark* could have been crafted to support. *Clement* and *Secret Gospel* are not only fifteen years too late, but, as many reviewers noted with bewilderment, they contain many ideas that have almost nothing to do with the actual text of *Secret Mark*. Thus, when Quesnell wondered about the relationship between *Secret Mark* and those ideas, Smith pounced, forcefully concluding, "it cannot be supposed that I concocted the text to support the theory."[24] Smith was quite correct, because his later theory is a trap for the unwary, designed to obscure what the text supports.[25] The proper method requires comparing the text of *Secret Mark* with his prior writings.

Of course *Secret Mark* supports the *sphragis* to his earlier writings. *Secret Mark's* coupling of Mark's "mystery of the kingdom of God" with a forbidden sexual relationship supports Smith's earlier linkage in 1951 of Mark 4:11 with forbidden sexual relationships. *Theodore's* exposition of Clement of Alexandria's secrecy over such relationships supports Smith's connection between Clement of Alexandria's views on secrecy and sexual practices which he published just a few months before his second visit to Mar Saba.

More substantively, *Secret Mark* also supports the criticisms he expressed in his 1955 review of Vincent Taylor's commentary on Mark. For instance, in his discussion of Mark 2:5, Smith conjectured that a "source with other Johannine traits" lay behind Mark's account of the healing of the paralytic.[26] *Secret Mark's* own version of the Johannine raising of Lazarus lends support to such a source. But the version of Lazarus in *Secret Mark* does not merely support Smith's conjectures about Mark's sources, it also supports Smith's indictment of Taylor:

> It is for apologetic motives that Taylor is willing to preserve the faults of nineteenth-century exegesis (notably its overemphasis on insignificant details), and even to revive those of the eighteenth century (notably its rationalistic 'explanations' of the miracles). It is because of his preoccupation with apologetics that he does not notice these faults are contradictory: On the one hand he finds 'vivid' details even where they do not exist and takes every vivid detail as a proof of 'primitive' tradition; on the other, he supposes this primitive tradition has fundamentally misunderstood the facts it faithfully reported.[27]

In particular, Smith focused on how Taylor handled Mark's miracles, which usually involved a rational, naturalistic explanation that accepts the truth of about as many factual details as possible in the miracle stories, yet permits denial of their supernaturalism. For example, in the healing of the paralytic (Mark 2:1-12), Taylor proposed that the paralysis was both psychologically caused and cured.[28] In the raising of the daughter of Jairus (Mark 5:21-24, 35-43), Taylor suggested that the little girl could well have been in a "trance-like sleep," not dead at all.[29] Yet Smith sensed a fundamental self-contradiction in Taylor's willingness to defend the historicity of the accidents but not the essence of Mark's narrative:

> So Mk.'s 'narrative is everywhere credible' (p. 318) as to everything but what Mk. meant to narrate. Clearly, this position is the product, not of criticism, but of the conflict of two apologetic techniques—to defend Mk. directly by accepting his stories, and to defend him indirectly by getting rid of his miracles.[30]

For the healing of the paralytic and the raising of Jairus's daughter, Smith argued that the details of these miracles should not be accepted as historical. Specifically, Smith suggested that a source having "Johannine traits" invented the vivid details: "But if it is a Johannine trait, what lies behind it is probably allegory or deliberate Johannine obfuscation, not psychological diagnosis."[31] Concerning Mark's account of the raising of the little girl, which surrounds the account of the woman in the crowd having an issue of blood, Smith wrote the following:

> [Quoting Taylor] ". . . the vivid portraiture of Jairus" (p. 285: There is no portraiture at all. T. tries to see it in vs. 22, but can only remark, ad loc., 'In the greatness of his distress he casts aside his dignity and falls at the feet of Jesus.' This is not portraiture, but pure convention, see προσπίπτω, 3.11; 5.33; 7.25 and προσκυνέω, 5.6, also παρακαλέω, 1.40 5.10,

12, 17, 18; 6.56; 7.32; 8.22) "and his agonized cry for help" (also conventional, cf. 7.32; 8.22; 16.18) "the incident of the woman on the way to the house" (probably added from some other source . . .) &c. T. thinks the interruption by the woman happened as told, especially because of 'while he was still speaking' in vs. 35. "In view of the comparative absence of connecting-links of this kind in Mk, it is reasonable to infer that the connexion is historical" (p. 289). But, granting that the final redactor of Mk. did not usually invent connections, it does not follow that he never did, still less that no splicing took place before the material reached his hands.[32]

Secret Mark's version of the raising of Lazarus supports Smith's several ways of declining to credit the accuracy of its factual details. In the version of the raising of Lazarus in Secret Mark, there was no miracle; when Jesus came to the tomb where the young man was, he was met with "a great cry," not the great stench of John 11:39. However, the naturalistic explanation for the raising found in Secret Mark does not maximize the number of true factual details in the Lazarus account, but instead incriminates the author of John 11:39 as deliberately obfuscating what really happened. Furthermore, Secret Mark also contains the words Smith earlier argued was not "portraiture" but "pure convention," including προσκυνέω ("she prostrated herself before Jesus") and παρακαλέω ("began to beseech him"). Secret Mark has the agonized cry for help too: "a great cry was heard from the tomb." Secret Mark even spliced two stories together—the raising of the young man and the nocturnal initiation—a feature of Mark's narrative about which Smith disputed Taylor's too eager willingness to conclude its historicity.

The raising of the young man in Secret Mark goes beyond supporting Smith's specific methodological quarrels with Vincent Taylor; it extends to Smith's broader indictment of Taylor's apologetics:

The passages discussed are sufficient for a clear picture not only of Taylor's book, but of the sort of NT scholarship it represents: the work of determined apologists. . . . What are these apologetic motives? To defend both the historical reliability of Mk. and the liberal Protestant picture of Jesus. . . . His book is thus a monument to his piety no less than to his scholarship.[33]

Smith's beliefs and opinions about the piety of the Establishment were long held and have been recorded in the biographical entries and memorials by his colleagues and students. Albert Baumgarten, one of Smith's students, elaborated on Smith's attitudes in the *Dictionary of Biblical Interpretation* in this way:

Early in his career S. left the church, characterizing the position he came to adopt as atheism: Belief in divine intervention in human affairs is not a valid basis for historical scholarship. He enjoyed provoking the conventionally faithful, proposing reconstructions of the past that opposed the narrative promoted by Jewish and Christian orthodoxies, and delighted in denouncing pseudo-orthodoxy—statements of faith masquerading as scholarship.[34]

Other portraits of Smith are consistent with this. For example, William M. Calder, III, wrote the following of Smith: "He delighted in outraging the pretentiously pious and had a keen sense for justice that made him fearless before the foe. 'Thank God I have tenure,' he said to a 'Times' reporter. He kindled heated discussion at scholarly gatherings and cheerfully collected threatened libel suits."[35] Shaye Cohen's picture is similar:

Smith never tired of discomforting the faithful. An ordained Episcopalian priest who left the church (but was never defrocked), Smith well knew that portrait of Jesus the Magician . . . was far from the respectable, rational, middle-class Christianity of most of his readers. . . . Smith reveled in this.[36]

Secret Mark supports not only Smith's love of controversy but also his favorite target. It was written during the 1950s, during an especially oppressive moment in American history when mainline ministers were urging the police to crack down on gay men gathered in public parks.[37] What could be more upsetting to the Establishment in this historical moment than the intimation, revealed in an ancient text by the author of the oldest gospel, that they are crucifying Jesus Christ all over again?

In Smith's scholarly obituary, Calder wrote that Smith's 1957 dissertation "was the first of many studies calculated to enrage the Establishment, Jewish or Christian, but far too intelligent and erudite to be dismissed as simply annoying."[38] Though not what Calder intended, it is difficult to find a more fitting description of Morton Smith's *Secret Mark*.

Needless to say, the desire to skewer the Establishment must not be over exaggerated, because it would otherwise be impossible to explain why Smith so carefully salted all those clues confessing to his hoax. Smith was a complex individual, and Calder observed that "the central contradiction in his life" was that he "was an articulate conservative . . . who mercilessly humiliated the Establishment."[39] Even as one part of him succumbed to fraud in lashing out against his enemies at one of the most vulnerable times in his life, another part of him, devoted to scholarship, could not permit the fake to stand for all time. Smith's hair-splitting avoidance of affirmative misstatements of fact in his publications about *Secret Mark* belies his anxiety over the ethics of this project. The scholar in him had to make his confession, even if its premature disclosure would have been at great personal and professional risk to himself. That is why Morton Smith's secret was a hoax, not a forgery.

That Smith seemingly took his "secret" to the grave does not run counter to conclusion that *Secret Mark* was his hoax. He enjoyed the ensuing battle of wits. He could have reckoned that, if "scholars of more piety than intelligence"[40] failed to pass his test, then they deserved to be stuck with this uncom-fortable text that negated their claims about what the Bible means. More probable, however, is that Smith rationalized that he did indeed disclose his secret but on his own terms, giving him the power that he lacked elsewhere in his life.

If Smith was motivated partly by malice against his oppo-nents, it is ironic that exposure of Smith's hoax may end up hurting mainly those who trusted him. Those hostile to what *Secret Mark* had to say simply relied on Quesnell's dismissal of Smith's text on a technicality, and many did. A fig leaf to be sure, but necessary cover from being exposed as fools. On the other hand, the people whose work will be called into question are those who trusted Smith but ignored the red flags surround-ing *Secret Mark*. But scholarship is ultimately about truth, not about faith in others. Come to think of it, that is what Smith spent his career trying to teach. Smith's last laugh from the grave is also his last lesson.

The full implications of Morton Smith's legacy for biblical scholarship remain to be seen, but one immediate result is clear. The bibliography of Morton Smith's published writings should be augmented to include a letter written in Greek around 1958 under the pseudonym "Clement."

7

The Anatomy of an Academic Hoax

Scholars have been creating a Jesus in their own image since the quest for the historical Jesus began more than two hundred years ago. For example, Albert Schweitzer once noted that the nineteenth-century quest produced one liberal, Protestant Jesus after another, much like the liberal, Protestant Germans who were engaged in the quest. Even today, some conceptions of the historical Jesus, such as the traveling Cynic philosopher that is popular among some North American professors, are suspected of being more reflective of today's anxieties in academia than first-century conditions. Accordingly, it should not be surprising, perhaps even inevitable, that Morton Smith came up with a Jesus that was very much like him. Smith would neither be the first nor the last to do so, but the key to understanding *Secret Mark* lies in understanding the Jesus that Smith created in his own image.

Smith's Jesus, of course, was *Jesus the Magician*. Although Smith's 1976 contribution to the quest for the historical Jesus explored how magicians were viewed in antiquity, Smith's hoaxing is best understood by an analogy to modern-day magicians—as masters of misdirection. Like the stage magician, the hoaxer depends on the ability to induce the audience to suspend its disbelief and accept the illusion for reality. Thus, one of the keys to understanding *Secret Mark* is to understand the role of misdirection.

Misdirection is the technique of causing the audience's attention to be distracted from the anomalies that would defeat the illusion. The first requirement is that the illusion must be plausible to the audience, and in the biblical studies field this means that a supposedly ancient text must be found in an ancient language in pre-modern handwriting. This requirement is sufficient by itself to filter out the vast majority of attempted biblical hoaxes, for example, the nineteenth-century *Unknown Life of Jesus*, which was supposedly written in Tibetan but only known through Nicholas Notovitch's Russian notes.[1] Likewise, the 1970s *Talmud Jmmanuel* known to UFOlogists can never be taken seriously by biblical scholars—its archetype is a German-language version claimed to have been translated from a destroyed Aramaic text. *Secret Mark*, by contrast, is a rare example of a modern biblical hoax written in ancient Greek. It has a plausibility lacking almost every other hoax attempt.

One of the central principles of misdirection is that the audience looks where the magician looks, and this applies to *Secret Mark* as well. For example, a magician will stare at the right hand to direct attention away from what the left hand is doing. This principle explains the large amount of irrelevant material in *Clement* and *Secret Gospel* including the nocturnal baptism, ascent into the heavens, and the exhaustive compilation of late and historically worthless *testimonia* on the Carpocratians. None of this information is directly relevant to the authenticity of *Secret Mark* but all of this information is useful for diverting scholars to focus their attention on matters unrelated to the authenticity of *Secret Mark*. This principle also explains why Smith dispersed the little information that was relevant to assessing *Secret Mark*'s authenticity into such hard-to-reach places as an obscure periodical published in Jerusalem translated into modern Greek. Smith understood the psychology of his peers well and was able to conceal some important information even in the non-scholarly, "popular" edition, *Secret Gospel*.

Sometimes, however, an anomaly may be so glaring that distracting the audience's attention away from it can be impossible. The best way to hide such an anomaly is to make it appear ordinary. For example, if a magician cannot conceal a trapdoor on the floor of the stage, then the trapdoor could be hidden in plain sight by putting a lot of fake trapdoors on the stage floor. Smith used this technique for *Secret Mark* by asking his colleagues to find as many problems with the *Clement* letter as possible and compiling them in his commentary. Thus, the serious problems with the letter were indiscriminately mixed in with a large number of insignificant issues.

Nevertheless misdirection is not a foolproof technique. It does not generally work on people unwilling to suspend disbelief who are alerted to the possibility of deception. Smith's original success with his colleagues in authenticating the paleography and style of the Clement letter may thus be due to their not realizing that a colleague they personally knew would try to hoax them in that way. Accordingly, *Secret Mark* exposes the role of the faith in academia. Philosophers have argued for centuries to what extent faith and reason are means to understanding reality. Since the Enlightenment, reason has generally won out in the academy, at least explicitly. But the very success of reason in generating knowledge has increased the role of faith, if only in the form of trusting other humans. A specialist in one field has to trust experts from other fields. Smith was able to exploit this faith in others by having paleographers give on-the-spot opinions on the appearance of Greek handwriting. Neither Smith nor the contents of *Theodore* alerted them to the possibility of forgery because (except for Arthur Darby Nock) Smith's experts for identifying eighteenth-century Greek handwriting were not experts about either Clement of Alexandria, who was rarely copied in that era, or pre-Markan gospel traditions. When it came time for the Clement scholars to look at the contents of *Theodore*, they were not considering the possibility of a recent forgery because of the conclusions of Smith's handwriting experts, and they rightly decided that the Clementine style exceeded the capabilities of eighteenth-century and earlier forgers. It is telling that, of all those Smith consulted, Nock was the one who voiced the strongest suspicions about the authenticity of *Theodore*—he was knowledgeable in all of the fields on which the *Secret Mark* compositions touched.

More difficult to explain, however, is the acceptance of *Secret Mark* by many in the academy even after Quesnell pointed out much of the misdirection in Smith's books. When the warning signs of deception are present, the effectiveness of misdirection then depends to a large extent on the complicity of the target audience. For example, the people attending a magic show expect there to be misdirection, but the audience is willing to suspend some measure of disbelief in order to be entertained in a context where it is safe to be deceived. In hoaxing the academy, however, scholars and scientists are not so willing to suspend their skepticism in their professional roles and especially not for amusement. Nevertheless, there are other vulnerabilities, as Harold Love explained:

> The first aid to spotting a fake is that it is usually a little too good to be true. What is provided has to be something so desirable to the victim, or the public, that normal scepticism is suspended: something either long desired or that provides support for a passionately held theory. *Qui vult decepi decipiatur*. It is for this reason that many shamelessly inept fakes have had long and successful lives. . . . When the ideological moment that brought forth the fake has passed it should be easier to see it as the product of contrivance.[2]

Thus, the success of an academic hoax crucially depends on its ability to tap into a deep-seated need among society's experts for assessing authenticity. The more unaware the experts are of their deep desires, the more effective the deception will be.

The Piltdown Man hoax, arguably the most successful academic hoax of modern times, is a good illustration of this, showing that scientists can be hoaxed as well as scholars in the humanities.[3] Prior to WWI, England competed with France and Germany on everything, including paleoanthropology, the study of early human ancestors. France had her cave paintings and Germany had the Neanderthals. Even though England had the first recognized dinosaur fossil, no early human remains were found in England. England's position changed dramatically, starting in 1908 when Charles Dawson, an amateur fossil hunter, found a fossil with an ape-like jaw and a human-like skull, having an age that made it the oldest human-like ancestor. This discovery not only put England on the map in anthropology but it provided stunning confirmation of Charles Darwin's theories at a time in which they were still racked with controversy in learned society. Dawson and Arthur Smith Woodward, the scientist at the British Museum who validated the remains, became famous. Some scientists, however, were initially skeptical, but they had difficulty explaining their skepticism and, in any case, they were denied access to the Piltdown remains on the grounds of their immense value. Eventually, a second Piltdown discovery closed off the early debate. The passage of time and the discovery of other early human remains, however, steadily marginalized Piltdown Man because, unlike the Piltdown Man, they had a human-like jaw and an ape-like skull. Piltdown Man was almost completely ignored in the early 1950s when a young scientist decided to take another look at the physical remains with a new fluorine-dating technique. Not only did the new technique prove Dawson and Woodward wrong, but the scientist also discovered obvious signs of forgery (such as artificial abrasion on its teeth) that should never have been missed in the first place.

There are differences between the Piltdown Man hoax and *Secret Mark*. The former involved the forgery of an artifact, not a text, and the Piltdown hoaxer never actually confessed. Nevertheless, the reception of the Piltdown Man bears many resemblances to that of *Secret Mark*. The initial enthusiasm over Piltdown Man led to controversy, then to increasing marginalization as newer discoveries show how poorly the fake fits with developing theories, and finally to very belated looks at the physical evidence. The psychological factors driving the Piltdown Man hoax were strong: the desire to settle the contemporary quarrel between science and religion, the frustration over lack of early human fossils, pre-World War I nationalism, and even personal ambition. When the hoax was uncovered, most of these factors had abated. By the 1950s, evolution had won over creationism in the universities; the subsequent discoveries of Peking Man and *Australopithecus* provided a useful quantity and quality of real fossil evidence; the failures of World War I and II repudiated nationalism; and many of the people involved in the Piltdown excavations had died. Without the psychological forces to keep propping it up, Piltdown Man was doomed.

Scholars and scientists are sometimes so used to looking at ancient evidence that they can too easily forget to be as skeptical of their contemporaries. This is one advantage that biographers and journalists tend to have over those studying the distant past, and skepticism over contemporary sources is the first defense against being hoaxed. Even this skepticism can break down under the right combination of powerful forces. A recent example occurred in September 2004 during a heated presidential campaign, when CBS News failed to follow its own standards in authenticating a set of memos for its exposé of President George W. Bush's National Guard service. Many reasons conspired to cause them not to follow their own journalistic guidelines, including the excitement of finding a "smoking gun" memo that confirmed their theories after five years of looking, the time pressure of possibly being scooped, the high-stakes of the election, and perhaps the long running dispute between the anchorman and the president's family. No one is immune from being deceived when the emotional factors happen to fall into place.

These cases, of course, are extraordinary, both in their scope and in their rarity because the multiple psychological forces have to align themselves just right and reinforce each other in just the right way to overcome the skepticism built into these institutions. The precise alignment of these forces is as fragile as it is powerful, and a case in point is the undoing of an alleged "forgery ring" that had purportedly been producing fake artifacts for the past twenty years in Israel. This ring, whose members are currently scheduled to go on trial in September 2005, had been mainly involved with first-temple period artifacts, when the kingdoms of Israel and Judea were at their height. These artifacts appealed to their victims, usually wealthy collectors, because they tended to confirm the historical, political claims within the Hebrew Bible. This apparent confirmation of such claims had a deep emotional resonance, because, in the mindset of such collectors and many others, Israel's legitimacy—if not her existence—unavoidably depends on whether archaeology confirms or denies the political claims of the Hebrew Bible. Forgers have been tapping into these emotional needs by providing the evidence that controlled archaeological digs otherwise have been slow in revealing.

The archaeological program into the first-temple period is absolutely vital within the ideological matrix of the present-day Middle East. This can be seen in how looters, not forgers, have typically been viewed as the more serious problem, because looters could potentially steal what little valuable evidence there is. Forgery is less worrisome because it might even reduce the demand for looting by artificially increasing the supply of ancient artifacts. As long as the prevalence of forged artifacts is not so great as to undermine the credibility of the entire archaeological program, preventing looting over forgery is a better allocation of scarce resources.

When the forgery ring turned its attention to producing a Christian artifact, however, the ring's careful plans fell apart. The artifact in question is the so-called "James ossuary," a limestone box that held the bones of a person supposedly identified by its inscription as "James, son of Joseph, brother of Jesus."[4] Unlike the other artifacts, the James ossuary did not have the same array of ideological forces behind it and was much weakened as a result. It is a second-temple artifact, not a first-temple one, and it does nothing to bolster perceptions of the historical legitimacy of the Jewish state. It also failed to fit the theological needs of its Christian audience. It is somewhat uncomfortable for Roman Catholics because the inscription may be understood to contradict, though not explicitly, the doctrine of the perpetual virginity of Mary. An artifact about James is also a poor fit for Protestants because James is on the wrong side of Paul in the Grace vs. Law debate that has historically defined the Protestant Reformation. Finally, the historicity of James is not in serious dispute, because it is supported by both the New Testament and the first-century Jewish historian Flavius Josephus.

One of the keys to a successful deception is that the fake has to appear so good to the intended victim that the victim is afraid of finding out it is not true and refuses to check. Almost no forgery can survive serious scrutiny, and the James ossuary was not as well ideologically positioned to avoid the scrutiny of watch dog agencies in comparison with the first-temple era fakes. Indeed, the actions of the ossuary's collector, such as not remembering when he purchased it and his shipping it to Canada, so worried the authorities as a looting case that they started investigating the ossuary and everything else the collector did.

Most of the deep-seated psychological reasons explained above for being willing to suspend disbelief about a particular fake have been ideological, and the academy can defend itself against ideological biases by increasing the diversity of its members. For example, scholars from different class backgrounds, from different countries, and of different genders, religions, and races, will respond differently to a fake's emotional appeals. Some may be enticed, but others will not be so tempted to follow the hoaxer's misdirection. A lack of diversity in the academy makes the academy more vulnerable to deception, though the price may be that consensus of any sort could be harder to achieve.

But ideology alone does not fully explain the relative success of *Secret Mark* because of the delay between its creation and publication. More specifically, *Secret Mark* had a number of components that would have appealed to liberal Protestants of the 1950s who were open to evidence for Jesus outside of the New Testament, willing to entertain notions of ecclesiastical censorship, and progressive enough to contemplate a limited variety of non-supernatural explanations for the miracle accounts. In the 1950s, they were still shocked by homosexuality. Thus, for its target audience, *Secret Mark* was both too appealing and too shocking to ignore. That was in 1958, but Smith did not publish his text until 1973.

A lot changed over this fifteen years. On the one hand, the "New Quest for the Historical Jesus" had gained ground with increased focus on Jesus' sayings, not his miracles. Thus, sources such as the *Gospel of Thomas* and the hypothetical collection of Jesus' sayings called Q became more important, while *Secret Mark*'s focus on narrative made itself irrelevant. On the other hand, 1973 was four years after Stonewall and at the beginning of the gay rights movement. The liberal Protestants so targeted to be challenged by *Secret Mark* were becoming less uncomfortable with homosexuality with each passing year, not enough for *Secret Mark* to be too appealing to ignore but sufficiently less shocking so that it could be more easily considered negligible. Meanwhile, *Secret Mark*

continued to lack any appeal for religious traditionalists. The
kind of person *Secret Mark* was designed to target was becoming extinct.

Nevertheless, *Secret Mark* continued to persist even as it was
feeding fewer ideological needs. What about *Secret Mark* is still
too good to be true? Bart D. Ehrman put his finger on a possible answer:

> It is the first shared assumption that I find most troubling,
> however—the view that we should stop asking if the
> Clementine letter was a modern forgery and acknowledge its
> utility for understanding second-century Christianity. And
> *why* should we do this?[5]

Secret Mark persists because it is still useful, not for the pur-
poses for which it was originally created, but because it continues to satisfy some current needs. *Secret Mark* is still being used
as an apt, even iconic illustration of the instability of gospel
traditions and their texts in the second century, or even to
make the point that religious scholars still cannot give a controversial text a fair shake. Scholars continue to use *Secret
Mark* for its iconic value even as they duly footnote the doubts
about *Secret Mark*.

Having a balanced portfolio of different life experiences and
philosophies among the faculty, can diversify away the academy's risk of being deceived for ideological reasons, but the his-
torical-critical enterprise will always have an inherent
vulnerability: good history is hard to do well. The traces of the
past, which ancient writings reveal and which now constitute
our body of evidence for history, was originally produced to
meet contemporary needs with little thought for the future.
They were created for specific reasons that were relevant in
their specific places and times. To the extent that writings from
the past contemplated the future, their authors did so on their
own terms, not on ours, and they framed issues based on their
sensibilities, not ours. In fact, those who created the artifacts
and documents that historians now use as sources had no

inkling about today's technical issues in the practice of historical criticism and could not answer the questions even if they wanted to. How could they? The questions that are relevant today depend in large part on the nature of the surviving evidence. As scholars discover and analyze more evidence, old questions are answered and new questions are raised.

As a result, historians have to treat sources from the past not as neutral observers but as hostile witnesses, who are not interested in answering today's questions but are intent on pursuing their own agendas. As with hostile witnesses, they have to be cross-examined and their testimony must be as independently corroborated as possible. Teasing out the implications of the data to answer our modern questions is a difficult endeavor that takes a lot of hard work, attention to detail, rigor, and, frankly, luck. To make matters worse, it is not always clear ahead of time whether enough information has survived to make that effort pay off.

On the other hand, fakes are easier to handle because they appear as sympathetic observers willing to answer today's questions. The modern faker already knows the questions that people are demanding to have answered and can tailor his or her creations to fit that need directly—certainly much better than the scraps of the genuine evidence historians are used to dealing with. In other words, hoaxes and forgeries provide, in one neat and tidy package, the illusory promise of answering contemporary questions. This illusion comes at a price, a price that the faker wants to extract. When usefulness trumps truth, scholars are in the danger of paying a terrible price.

"History," as Smith put it, "is by definition the search for the most probable explanations of preserved phenomena," knowing full well that "truth is necessarily stranger than history" (*Secret Gospel* 148). Smith was referring to his historical reconstruction of the transmission of *Secret Mark* based on a disingenuously limited set of evidence, but his statement is true in a different sense as well. History is much more than the antiquarian's

interest in what exactly happened when, though that information is essential. History is about broadening our understanding
about ourselves as humans, to learn which parts of the human
experience may be universal and which parts may be socially
constructed. In this way, history is like visiting a foreign country. Both allow us to study different points of view about the
human experience. Going to a foreign country and learning
about different customs allows us to identify what parts of our
own experience are culturally specific. Similarly, studying
period-specific texts allows us to identify what parts of our own
experience are more accidental than essential. This is the reason why historical fakes are so pernicious—hoaxers are no less
immune from producing a historical Jesus that looks like themselves than scholars are. Instead of being able to broaden our
horizons with their own period-specific point of view, contemporary fakes merely reinforce our prejudices. The historical
hoax is thus the equivalent of a tourist trap—more comfortable
to visit, even exciting, but a lot less informative and definitely
misleading. Yet the hoax's relevance to the contemporary visitor is also its fundamental weakness. What was used to make
the hoax relevant will become more foreign to the next gener-
ation and the period-specific truth of the hoax will stand out.

Therefore, truth is necessarily more foreign than history.

Appendix

Extracts from Smith's 1960 Catalog

[p. 110] GREEK MANUSCRIPTS IN THE MONASTERY OF ST. SABA

According to a translation from the English by the bl. hierom. Constantine Michaelides.

Beginning the report of the manuscripts in the monastery of St. Saba, I would recognize my obligation to express my sincere thanks to His Beatitude the Patriarch of Jerusalem Benedict, who kindly granted me permission to stay at the monastery, study, research, and publish my findings. Thanks are also owed to the Blessed Sacristy of the Holy Sepulcher Archimandrite Kyriakos,* to the blessed Steward of St. Saba Archimandrite Seraphim and to all the blessed fathers and brothers of the monastery, of whose hospitality and assistance made my stay as pleasant as it was fruitful.

Anyone who has visited the monastery of St. Saba must come away with the deep impression of the serenity of the place, of its magnificence and holiness and that to have the honor of living a little while in St. Saba, that is still not inferior both to the examination of manuscripts and to whatever we describe here below.

* The author wrote this report before the death of the ever-memorable Elder Kyriakos.

[p. 111] The following catalog was principally made about whatever Greek manuscripts are found now in the monastery. In addition to these there are one Turkish manuscript and twelve others, comprising quite a few extracts of books in the Cyrillic alphabet and a similar number of Romanian manuscripts with Latin characters. When I came to prepare the present catalog of manuscripts, I thought it would be good to number some of them without comments (3–5 and 7–8). All the manuscripts are found in the library, in the Tower, except any of whose places are referred to in the present catalog.

. . .

[p. 119] 22. (18th cen.), paper, dimensions 200 x 148 x 31, 17 sheets. "The Summer," viz. lives of the Saints with feast days, falling between the 1st of March and 31st of October. The main part of the work is a printed edition of Venice (1656). The first 11 sheets and the final 6 were restored by a hand of the 18th century. A caption gives the writer as Joseph. The present book in our catalog includes not just an example of a completed manuscript (of which the library contains rather much), but also for this reason it is particularly rich in notes by previous owners or users: f. 1 r., M. Madiotes (handwriting of the 20th cen.). The monk Dionysios, Archimandrite, (handwriting of the 19th cen.); . . . Anobos monk of the Holy Sepulcher (18th cen. ?); f. 1v., the monk Modestus the Holy Sabbite, 1916; f. 2r., the priest James, monk in the Holy Laura of St. Sabas (one pen stroke, 18th cen. ?). "This collection of the lives of the Saints through the summer time was given by me, the monk James to the monastery of St. Sabas, and anyone who takes it may have a curse of 318 God-bearing Fathers (of Nicaea) and the curse of St. Sabas. In the year 1756, 12 January.

The final sheet (r.), a Romanian writing with Latin characters, pertains to a brother of a certain Dionysios and is dated 1779. The final sheet (v.), Doukas, son of the blessed Panagiotis the tailor (ampatzes). With them also conforms a number of notes, of which most concern discussing the great storm in January and February 1779. Ultimately, the binding is a composition of pages from older Georgian manuscripts,[1] perhaps Armenian, Arabic, Hebrew or Syriac and Greek of the 10th and [p. 121] 11th centuries.[1] This binding proves the availability of older manuscript material according to the time when this work was bound a second time, probably at the beginning of the 18th century, given that the latest of the writing on top appears to be that of James of the date 1756.

[p. 120] 1. For the reading of the Georgian manuscripts I thank Rev. Fr. Bridgeman, dean of the Church of the Holy Trinity in New York, Prof. Der Nersessian and Mr. Zizichvili, librarian of Dumbarton Oaks.

[p. 121] 1. The Greek contains passages from the books of the Holy Liturgy.

. . .

[p. 251] 65. (18th cen.), paper, dim. 198 x 148 x 23, two sheets. Excerpt from a letter of Clement of Alexandria, addressed to a certain Theodore. Written on both pages of the last sheet of *Epistolae genuinae, S. Ignatii Martyris* (ed. I. Voss, Amsterdam, 1646) and at the top of another following sheet, used as binding paper. The page that bears the title of the book is lost, but Voss signed the dedication and I could identify the edition of this by comparing the photographs of pages 2 and 318 with those of the pages of a copy of the same book, kept in the Union Theological Seminary. The 2 sheets of binding in question were probably contemporaneous with the publication of the book. But for an accurate dating of the writing, I owe thanks to Messrs. A. *Angelou* and K. *Dimaras*, of the Greek National Foundation, A. *Delatte*, professor of the University of Liège, G. *Kournoutos*, of the Ministry of Education of Greece, M. *Manousakas*, of the Greek National Archives, professor A. *Nock*, of Harvard University, M. *Richard*, of the Institute of Research and History of Texts, V. *Skouvaras*, professor of the Gymnasium of Volos, G. *Soulis*, of the library of Dumbarton

Oaks, and *P. Topping*, of the Library of Gennadeion, in Athens. All of the foregoing studied the [p. 252] photocopies of the manuscript in question and gave me their independent opinions with respect to the dating of the writing. Their opinions varied. And while Mr. Kournoutos accepts that it was written around the end of the 17th cen. or the beginning of the 18th cen., professors *Delatte, Skouvaras,* and Mr. *Topping* accept its dating around the end of the 18th cen. or the beginning of the 19th cen., but all generally agree for a dating in the 18th cen.

Other excerpts of the letters of Clement are known to us (See the Berlin edition ed. O. *Stahlin* [*sic*], vol. III, pp. 223–24), but it does not follow from this that the genuineness of the excerpt to Theodore is established, which must be compared with the style of other works of Clement. Thus the debate as to the authentication of the contents of the letter to Theodore must wait until the completion of the inquiry.

. . .

[p. 256] 76. (20th cen., 1910), paper, dim. 250 x 200 x 1, 7 sheets written on one side. A catalog of books of the library in the year 1910. 191 titles of books were recorded and written without comments. I discovered this catalog during the final day of my stay in the monastery and I did not have the time to examine it.

Apart from the aforementioned manuscripts present in the library, in the tower, there are 20 liturgical manuscripts all of the 19th and 20th centuries and two folders full of manuscript material. One of the folders is of paper and mainly contains liturgical matter: music, hymns and prayers. The other, of leather, mainly contains old matter, lives of the saints, personal writings and foreign language phrase books, but also some sermons and excerpts of the regulations and other matter, but most of them composite. Very few fragments appear to be before the 17th cen. The existence of other manuscripts in other places in the monastery is also possible and I am not surprised if a big discovery of other manuscripts would happen within or near the monastery.

Notes

Introduction

1   Morton Smith, *Clement of Alexandria and a Secret Gospel of Mark* (Cambridge, Mass.: Harvard University, 1973), ix and 1. Essential details are found in the simultaneously published "popular" edition, Morton Smith, *The Secret Gospel: The Discovery and Interpretation of the Secret Gospel According to Mark* (New York: Harper & Row, 1973), ix, 1–17. References to these works are made inline as *Clement* and *Secret Gospel*, respectively.

2   Smith identifies the book as Isaac Voss, *Epistulae* [sic] *genuinae S. Ignatii Martyris* (Amsterdam: J. Blaeu, 1646). The spelling of the first word is *Epistolae*, with an *o*.

3   Guy G. Stroumsa, "Comments on Charles Hedrick's Article: A Testimony," *JECS* 11 (2003): 147–53, at 147–48. Stroumsa is the last western scholar alive to have seen the manuscript.

4   Charles W. Hedrick, with Nikolaos Olympiou, "Secret Mark: New Photographs, New Witnesses," *Fourth R* 13, no. 5 (2000): 3–16 (hereinafter "New Photographs"). Fortunately, Hedrick and Olympiou were able to publish color photographs of the manuscript taken in the 1970s.

5   Shawn Eyer, "The Strange Case of the Secret Gospel According to Mark: How Morton Smith's Discovery of a Lost Letter by Clement of Alexandria Scandalized Biblical Scholarship," *Alexandria: The Journal for the Western Cosmological Traditions* 3 (1995): 103–29.

6 Eyer, "Strange Case." See Joseph A. Fitzmyer, "How to Exploit a Secret Gospel," *America*, June 23, 1973, 570–72, at 571: "from the brow of Morton Smith . . . from my less balding pate." See also the survey in Morton Smith, "Clement of Alexandria and Secret Mark: The Score at the End of the First Decade," *HTR* 75 (1982): 449–61 (hereinafter "Score").

7 Quentin Quesnell, "The Mar Saba Clementine: A Question of Evidence," *CBQ* 37 (1975): 48–67; Morton Smith, "On the Authenticity of the Mar Saba Letter of Clement," *CBQ* 38 (1976): 196–99 (hereinafter "Authenticity"); and Quentin Quesnell, "A Reply to Morton Smith," *CBQ* 38 (1976): 200–203.

8 E.g., Helmut Koester, Response to Reginald H. Fuller, in *Longer Mark: Forgery, Interpolation, or Old Tradition?* (ed. W. Wuellner; Protocol of the Eighteenth Colloquy; Berkeley, Calif.: Center for Hermeneutical Studies, 1976); Helmut Koester, "History and Development of Mark's Gospel (From Mark to *Secret Mark* and 'Canonical' Mark)," in *Colloquy on New Testament Studies: A Time for Reappraisal and Fresh Approaches* (ed. Bruce Corley; Macon, Ga.: Mercer University Press, 1983); Helmut Koester, *Ancient Christian Gospels: Their History and Development* (Philadelphia: Trinity, 1990), 293–303; John Dominic Crossan, *Four Other Gospels: Shadows on the Contours of the Canon* (New York: Harper & Row, 1985; repr. Sonoma, Calif.: Polebridge, 1992), 61–83; and Hans-Martin Schenke, "The Mystery of the Gospel of Mark," *SecCent* 4 (1984): 65–82.

9 For example, Morton Smith, "Regarding *Secret Mark*: A Response by Morton Smith to the Account of Per Beskow," *JBL* 103 (1984): 624, responding to Per Beskow, *Strange Tales about Jesus: A Survey of Unfamiliar Gospels* (Philadelphia: Fortress, 1983). Smith's response was an advertisement in *JBL* paid by Beskow's publisher.

10 Shaye J. D. Cohen, "Morton Smith and Secret Mark," *Ioudaios*, July 11, 1995, n.p.: "As Smith's literary executor I went through his papers after his death in 1991. There was nothing that would indicate or imply that he forged the Secret Gospel. This, of course, hardly proves that he did not forge the whole thing, but,

if he did, he left no death-bed confession." ftp://ftp.lehigh.edu
/pub/listserv/ioudaios-l//archives/9507b. Accessed May 16, 2005.

11   E.g., Joel Marcus, *Mark 1–8: A New Translation with Introduction
and Commentary* (ABD 27; New York: Doubleday, 2000), 51: "It
is better to go along with Koester and treat Secret Mark—if it
ever existed—as a late edition of Mark that reveals the concern
for esotericism typical of second-century Alexandrian Christianity. Contrary to Koester, however, Secret Mark is more likely a
redaction of Canonical Mark than the other way around."

12   Larry W. Hurtado, *Lord Jesus Christ: Devotion to Jesus in Earliest
Christianity* (Grand Rapids: Eerdmans, 2003), 314–15 (footnotes
omitted).

13   A second-century dating seems to be the kiss-of-death for those
investigating the historical Jesus. See, e.g., John P. Meier, *A
Marginal Jew: Rethinking the Historical Jesus* (ABDL 1; New York,
Doubleday, 1991), 123: "These apocryphal gospels are very
important, but they belong in a study of the patristic Church
from the 2d to the 4th century. . . . There is nothing in here that
can serve as a source in our quest for the historical Jesus." Meier
has drawn controversy over his treatment of *Gospel of Thomas*,
not because of disagreement with his view about the value of second century apocryphal gospels, but because he placed Thomas
in the second century. Thomas is literally the exception that
proves the rule.

14   E.g., Michael J. Haren, "The Naked Young Man: a Historian's
Hypothesis on Mark 14,51–52," *Bib* 79 (1998): 525–31, at 531,
n. 23: "The so-called Secret Gospel of Mark would portray
Lazarus so dressed . . . but its evidence does not seem worth
adducing in view of the doubt that must be entertained . . . about
the authenticity of the letter of Clement in which it is commu-
nicated."

15   Most recently, Bruce M. Metzger, *Reminiscences of an
Octogenarian* (Peabody, Mass.: Hendrickson, 1997), 128–32; Bart
D. Ehrman, *Lost Christianities: The Battles for Scripture and the
Faiths We Never Knew* (Oxford: Oxford University Press, 2003),
67–89; and Robert M. Price, "Second Thoughts about the Secret
Gospel," *BBR* 14 (2004), 127–32. See also Donald Harman
Akenson, *Saint Saul: A Skeleton Key to the Historical Jesus*

(Oxford: Oxford University Press, 2000), 84–89, who expands upon his treatment in *Surpassing Wonder: The Invention of the Bible and the Talmuds* (Chicago: University of Chicago Press, 1998), 595–97.

16   Charles W. Hedrick, "The Secret Gospel of Mark: Stalemate in the Academy," *JECS* 11 (2003): 133–45 (hereinafter "Stalemate").

17   April D. DeConick, "The Original Gospel of Thomas," *VC* 56 (2002): 167–99, at 182. See also Margaret M. Mitchell, "Patristic Counter-Evidence to the Claim that 'The Gospels Were Written for All Christians'," *NTS* 51 (2005): 36–79, at 76 n. 113: "but this infamously debated document is by no means the only evidence of esoteric gospels in the early church."

18   Scott G. Brown, "The More Spiritual Gospel: Markan Literary Techniques in the Longer Gospel of Mark" (Ph.D. diss., U. Toronto, 1999); and Scott G. Brown, *Mark's Other Gospel: Rethinking Morton Smith's Controversial Discovery* (ESCJ 15; Ontario: Wilfrid Laurier University Press, 2005). The claim about Brown's doctoral dissertation being the first ever written on *Secret Mark* is on the back cover of *Mark's Other Gospel*.

19   Brown's few new arguments will be addressed later where relevant.

Chapter 1

1   Although the SBL style manual refers to *Secret Mark*, it does not include the letter to Theodore among Clement's works (*The SBL Handbook of Style: For Ancient Near Eastern, Biblical, and Early Christian Studies* [ed. Patrick H. Alexander et al.; Peabody, Mass.: Hedrickson, 1999], 84 and 244). Accordingly, the letter will be referred to as *Theodore* and abbreviated as *Theod.* Unless otherwise indicated, all citations and English translations of *Theodore* refer to the plate and line number of its *editio princeps* at *Clement* 448–52.

2   More specifically, he visited Mar Saba "[a]fter the Christmas season," i.e., after January 6, 1942 (*Secret Gospel* 1), "spent almost two months there" (4), and returned to Jerusalem "early in Lent" (6).

3   Morton Smith, *Maqbilot ben haBesorot le Sifrut haTanna'im* (Ph.D. Diss., Hebrew University, 1948); revised English translation,

Tannaitic Parallels to the Gospels (JBL Monograph Series 6; Philadelphia: Society of Biblical Literature 1951).

4   According to Julia Randall, archivist of the Virginia Theological Seminary, Smith served at St. Ambrose Mission in Philadelphia from 1945–1946 and at Mt. Calvary in Baltimore from 1946–1948 (pers. comm., May 11, 2005).

5   Morton Smith, "Σύμμεικτα: Notes on Collections of Manuscripts in Greece," Ἐπετηρὶς Ἑταιρείας Βυζαντιῶν Σπουδῶν [*Journal of the Society for Byzantine Studies*] 26 (1956): 380–93.

6   Stroumsa, "Comments," 150, citing a letter dated January 26, 1953.

7   William M. Calder, III, "Morton Smith†," *Gn* 64 (1992): 382–83.

8   Morton Smith, "Comments on Taylor's Commentary on Mark," *HTR* 48 (1955): 21–64. The commentary itself is Vincent Taylor, *The Gospel According to St. Mark: The Greek Text with Introduction, Notes, and Indexes* (London: Macmillan, 1952).

9   Smith, "Σύμμεικτα" and Morton Smith, "The Manuscript Tradition of Isidore of Pelusium," *HTR* 47 (1956): 205–10. See also Morton Smith, "An Unpublished Life of St. Isidore of Pelusium" in Εὐχαριστήριον (ed. G. Konidaris; Athens, 1958), based on a manuscript he inspected while at Brown.

10 Morton Smith, "The Description of the Essenes in Josephus and the Philosophumena," *Hebrew Union College Annual* 29 (1958): 273–313. In note 1, Smith thanked his colleagues at Drew, where he taught from 1956–1957, for interesting him in the material.

11 Morton Smith, "The Image of God: Notes on the Hellenization of Judaism, with Especial Reference to Goodenough's Work on Jewish Symbols," *Bulletin of the John Rylands Library* 40 (1958): 473–512, reprinted in Shaye J. D. Cohen, ed., *Studies in the Cult of Yahweh* (RGRW 130; Leiden: Brill, 1996), 1:116–49. The four citations are: "Image of God," 482, n. 2 = *Studies*, 1:124, n. 33; "Image of God," 501, n. 3 = *Studies*, 1:139, n. 110; "Image of God," 507, n. 5 = *Studies*, 1:145, n. 152, and "Image of God," 511, n. 5 = *Studies*, 1:148, n. 174.

12 Stroumsa, "Comments," 150.

13   Smith was forty-three when he visited Mar Saba (*Secret Gospel* 10), i.e., on or after May 28, 1958, since Smith was born May 28, 1915 (Calder, "Morton Smith†," 382).

14   Morton Smith, "Monasteries and their Manuscripts," *Archaeology* 13, no. 3 (1960): 175.

15   Smith, "Σύμμεικτα," 380–81, discussing nine manuscripts in Cephalonia he dated to the eighteenth century.

16   Morton Smith, "᾿Ελληνικὰ χειρόγραφα ἐν τῇ Μονῇ τοῦ ἁγίου Σάββα" ["Greek manuscripts in the monastery of St. Saba"] (trans. K. Michaelides, *Νέα Σιών* [*New Zion*] 52 [1960]): 251.

17   Sanka Knox, "A New Gospel Ascribed to Mark," *The New York Times*, December 30, 1960, and idem, "Expert Disputes 'Secret Gospel,' " *The New York Times*, December 31, 1960.

18   The fifteen-year delay between discovery and publication for *Secret Mark* and *Theodore* is not particularly unusual. Examples of similar delays in other texts are collected by Gerd Theissen and Annette Merz, *The Historical Jesus: A Comprehensive Guide* (trans. John Bowden; Minneapolis: Fortress, 1998), 19.

19   Robert M. Grant, "Morton Smith's Two Books," *ATR* 56 (1974): 58–65, at 59. Cf. also Pierson Parker, "An Early Christian Cover-up?" *The New York Times*, July 22, 1973: "if Professor Smith's conclusions seem wild (to some of us), he has nonetheless contributed richly to scholarship"; and Dennis Nineham, review of *The Secret Gospel*, *JTS* 27 (1976): 195–97, at 197: "It would be iniquity if the tenuousness of the line which links much of this speculation on the find at Mar Saba dissuaded scholars."

20   Paul J. Achtemeier, reviews of *Clement of Alexandria* and *The Secret Gospel*, *JBL* 93 (1974): 625–28, at 626.

21   Quesnell, "Mar Saba Clementine," 53.

Chapter 2

1   Quesnell, "Reply," 201.

2   Quesnell, "Reply," 201.

3   Cf. Smith, "Score," 451: "None of these studies contained any substantial argument to show that Clement could *not* have written the letter; they merely suggested reasons for thinking that someone else *might* have written it" (emphasis original).

4   Hedrick, "New Photographs," 9.

5   A point raised by Hedrick, "New Photographs," 6. One example, alluded to by Smith (*Clement* 289), is the epistle to Diognetus, whose text is only known now from transcriptions of a manuscript that perished in Strasbourg in 1870.

6   Bruce M. Metzger, "Literary Forgeries and Canonical Pseudepigrapha," *JBL* 91 (1972): 3–24 (the quotation is found at p. 4). See also, Wolfgang Speyer, *Die literarische Fälschung im heidnischen und christlichen Altertum: eine Versuch ihrer Deutung* (Munich: Beck, 1971), 13: "Täuschungsabsicht." Indeed, some of the most difficult fakes to detect are those not created to deceive, for example, scholarly reconstructions that are later misidentified or misattributed. See Gilbert Bagnani, "On Fakes and Forgeries," *Phoenix* 14 (1960): 228–44, at 236.

7   Anthony Grafton, *Forgers and Critics: Creativity and Duplicity in Western Scholarship* (Princeton: Princeton University Press, 1990), 67.

8   E.g., Richard Bauckham, "Pseudo-Apostolic Letters," *JBL* 107 (1988): 475, explaining that "the pseudepigraphical letter, by its very nature, requires a distinction between the supposed addressee(s) and the real readers."

9   See, e.g., Grafton, *Forgers and Critics,* 62: "Structural techniques . . . are necessary but not sufficient to a successful forgery. One further effort, as amorphous as it is important, must still be made: the creation of an air of verisimilitude and significance."

10   Harold Love, *Attributing Authorship: An Introduction* (Cambridge: Cambridge University Press, 2002), 184–85.

11   See Quesnell, "Mar Saba Clementine," 60, n. 30.

12   Gilbert Bagnani, "On Fakes and Forgeries," 234, characterizes a "true forgery" as *dolo malo et in sordidam mercedem.* Werner Helbig's forged inscription of the Praenestine fibula that neatly confirms his theories about the nature of archaic Latin may be an example done to gain an intellectual, rather than a pecuniary, advantage (Grafton, *Forgers and Critics,* 38). See also Philip Baldi, *The Foundation of Latin* (Trends in Linguistics Studies and Monographs 117; Berlin: Mouton de Gruyter, 1999), 125, n. 2: "Needless to say, such a trove of archaisms in a single source would make this specimen invaluable if it were authentic, which I am convinced it is not."

13   See, for example, Bagnani, "On Fakes and Critics," 235, calling a good hoax "a dangerous game to play. If the hoaxer is either so good that he deceives all the people . . . he may find himself hoist with his own petard."

14   Both Grafton, *Forgers and Critics*, 3–4, and Ehrman, *Lost Christianities*, 88–89.

15   Both of the following examples, Pfaff and Coleman-Norton, were cited in connection with *Secret Mark* by Quesnell, "Mar Saba Clementine," 57, nn. 11, 19, and 30. Though Grafton did not discuss *Secret Mark*, he mentioned both Pfaff (*Forgers and Critics*, 32) and Coleman-Norton (4–5).

16   The following discussion in this paragraph is based on Adolf Harnack, *Die Pfaff'schen Irenäus-Fragmente als fälschungen Pfaffs* (TU n. f. 5.3; Leipzig: Hinrichs, 1900), 1–69, at 9–10, references to which are made inline.

17   According to Grafton, Pfaff was one who "forged in part for idealistic reasons" (*Forgers and Critics*, 32); see also Smith, *Clement*, 85, n. 8.

18   Ehrman, *Lost Christianities*, 76–77.

19   This was the conclusion of Metzger, *Reminiscences of an Octogenarian*, 136–39.

20   Paul R. Coleman-Norton, "An Amusing *Agraphon*," *CBQ* 12 (1950): 439–49. In this paragraph, references to Coleman-Norton's article are made inline. Coleman-Norton has also been invoked in connection with *Secret Mark* by Ehrman, *Lost Christianities*, 69–70, and Quesnell, "Mar Saba Clementine," 54 n. 11.

21   Metzger, *Reminiscences of an Octogenarian*, 138 and Coleman-Norton, "Amusing *Agraphon*," 439–40, n. 4.

22   Metzger, "Literary Forgeries and Canonical Pseudepigrapha," 439 and *Reminiscences of an Octogenarian*, 139.

23   Quesnell, "Mar Saba Clementine," 60, n. 30.

24   See, e.g., R. Albert Mohler, Jr., "Modern Theology: The Disappearance of Hell," in *Hell Under Fire: Modern Scholarship Reinvents Eternal Punishment* (eds. Christopher W. Morgan and Robert A. Peterson; Grand Rapids: Zondervan, 2004), 15–42.

25   Smith, "Score," 456. The full sentence reads: "Now the mass of

factual data that had to be dealt with in evaluating the letter of Clement and Secret Mark was such that my full presentation, *Clement*, is a dreadfully complex book."

26 James H. Hunter, *The Mystery of Mar Saba* (Grand Rapids: Zondervan, 1940; repr. 1947).

27 Hunter, *Mystery of Mar Saba*, 280–83. This was suspicious to Price, "Second Thoughts about the Secret Gospel," 131.

28 The Greek text begins with "ΕΓΩΔΕΝΙΚΟΔΕΜΟΣΣΥΝΙΩ– ΣΗΟΑΠΟΑΡΙΜΑΘΑΙΑΣ . . ." which means "I, Nicodemus in company with Joseph of Arimathea . . ." (Hunter, *Mystery of Mar Saba*, plate facing title page).

29 Philip Jenkins, *Hidden Gospels: How the Search for Jesus Lost Its Way* (Oxford: University Press, 2001), 102. Jenkins likened Smith's claim to a hypothetical announcement of "an epoch-making paleontological find from the English site of Piltdown" (102).

30 Ehrman, "Response to Charles Hedrick's Stalemate," *JECS* 11 (2003): 162.

31 Ehrman, "Response," 162, paraphrasing Voss, *Epistulae genuinae S. Ignatii Martyris*, 318: "Plures enim paginas nugis istis implerat impudentissimus iste nebulo."

Chapter 3

1 Quesnell, "Mar Saba Clementine," 48.

2 See also Ehrman, "Response," 162: "We won't know until, if ever, the manuscript is found and subjected to a rigorous investigation, including testing the ink." See also Crossan, *Four Other Gospels*, 68: "The essential problem, then, is the lack of several independent studies of the original document by experts on Greek handwriting. Private responses to necessarily amateur photographs were quite good enough to start the process of verification but are utterly inadequate to conclude it. There are bound to be doubts about authenticity when the experts have only seen 'photographs of the manuscripts' (Smith 1973b: 1)."

3 The new color photographs published by Hedrick ("New Photographs") did not significantly extend our knowledge of the physical manuscript much beyond the size of the margins and

that the manuscript did indeed remain at Mar Saba after Smith left it in 1958.

4   The people consulted were: A. Angelou, C. Dimaras, A. Delatte, G. Kournoutos, M. Manousakas, A. D. Nock, M. Richard, V. Scouvaras, G. Soulis, and P. Topping (*Clement* 1).

5   Smith, "Authenticity," 196.

6   Smith, "Authenticity," 196 ("photographs") and Smith, " Ἑλληνικά," 252 (φωτοτυπέας = "Photostats" or "photocopies"), respectively.

7   Smith, "Authenticity," 196.

8   Thoroughly discussed by Quesnell, "Mar Saba Clementine," 48–53.

9   See generally, Charles Hamilton, *Great Forgers and Famous Fakes: The Manuscript Forgers of America and How They Duped the Experts* (2d. ed.; Lakewood, Colo.: Glenbridge, 1996); Katherine M. Koppenhaver, *Attorney's Guide to Document Examination* (Westport, Conn.: Quorum, 2002); Joe Nickell, *Detecting Forgery: Forensic Investigation of Documents* (Lexington: University Press of Kentucky, 1996); Joe Nickell, *Pen, Ink & Evidence: A Study of the Writing and Writing Materials for the Penman, Collector, and Document Detective* (New Castle, Del.: Oak Knoll, 2003); Albert S. Osborn, *Questioned Documents* (2d ed.; Albany: Boyd Printing, 1929); and Kenneth W. Rendell, *Forging History: The Detection of Fake Letters and Documents* (Norman: University of Oklahoma Press, 1994). I was also assisted by Julie C. Edison, a professional forensic document examiner who has given courtroom and deposition testimony in Virginia, Maryland, Connecticut, and Australia.

10   Osborn, *Questioned Documents*, 273–74. Osborn was acknowledged as an expert by Quesnell, "Mar Saba Clementine," 52, n. 9, and is still considered authoritative in court of law today according to expert examiner Edison.

11   Osborn, *Questioned Documents*, 294–95.

12   Osborn, *Questioned Documents*, 283. Osborn noted that "a jury within ten minutes returned a verdict that the two disputed signatures were not genuine."

13   Kenneth W. Clark, *Checklist of manuscripts in the libraries of the Greek and Armenian Patriarchates in Jerusalem, microfilmed for the*

Library of Congress, 1949–50, prepared under the direction of Kenneth W. Clark, director and general editor of the Jerusalem Expedition, 1949–50 (Washington, DC: Library of Congress, 1953).

14 In ὅλον (Figure 2A), δούλου and φιλάττων (Figure 2B), and πόλε- (Figure 2C).

15 In κλήμεντος (Figure 3A), ἐλευθερία (Figure 3D), ἀπῆλθεν (Figure 3E), and ἀληθῆ and φιλοσοφίαν (Figure 3F).

16 In ἐπιστολῶν (Figure 3A), πλανώμενοι (Figure 3B), and ἀληθὴς (Figure 3F).

17 In τῶν and τοῦ (Figure 3A) and τῶν (Figure 3B).

18 In τοῦ, σῶτερ, and φιλάττων (Figure 2B) and τοῦ (Figure 2C).

19 Cf. Akenson, Saint Saul, 88: "Morton Smith's big treatise . . . concludes with two very fuzzy photographs of the only known sighting of the great discovery: clearer pictures of the Loch Ness monster are available." Actually, the big treatise concludes with three photographs of the manuscript, and the fuzziness is due to the age of the paper when the ink was applied.

20 Joe Nickell, Detecting Forgery: Forensic Investigation of Documents (Lexington: University Press of Kentucky, 1996), 128.

21 Brown, Mark's Other Gospel, 26.

22 Brown, Mark's Other Gospel, 26: "Since we are dealing with two different sets of photographs taken twenty-three years apart under different lighting conditions and using different quality film, it is probably not possible to determine whether this fact has any significance."

23 Hedrick, "New Photographs," 10–11.

24 Nickell, Pen, Ink, & Evidence, 36.

25 Brown, Mark's Other Gospel, 27. Brown's confidence over identifying the color of the ink in the photographs is in stark contrast with his caution over the color of the browned edges.

26 Brown, Mark's Other Gospel, 27.

27 The lighter shaded portions in the black-and-white photographs are found where the pen was moving more quickly and depositing a lesser amount of ink.

28 Brown, Mark's Other Gospel, 27: "Although the ink depicted in the colour photos is the expected colour of oxidized iron or 'rust,' the paper on which the Letter to Theodore was written also

appears quite brown in Kallisto's photos." Brown's color terminology is confusing. The ink is darker than the paper, so the
"rust" color of the ink is actually a dark brown and the "quite
brown" for the paper, at least near the ink, is a deep yellow.

29   Akenson, *Saint Saul*, 85.

30   Quesnell, "Mar Saba Clementine," 54.

31   Personal email dated December 4, 2003 from Antiquariat
Thomas Rezek of Munich.

32   Smith, "Ἑλληνικά," 256; see also Smith, *Clement*, 290

33   My translation of "δεν εἶχον τὸν χρόνον νὰ τὸν ἐξετάσω" from
Smith, "Ἑλληνικά," 256.

34   Quesnell, "Mar Saba Clementine," 56.

35   Quesnell, "Mar Saba Clementine," 49–50.

36   Stroumsa, "Comments," 147.

37   More precisely, the physical dimensions of the Voss edition are
198 x 148 x 23 mm or $7\,^{3}/_{4}$" x 6" x $^{3}/_{4}$" (Smith, "Ἑλληνικά," 251,
but omitted from *Clement* or *Secret Gospel*).

38   Hedrick, "Stalemate," 140, n. 23: "This, of course, is only my
opinion, but during a visit to the monastery in 1990, I was
impressed that the conditions in the monastery, even at that
later time, would not have been favorable for such a forgery."
Nevertheless, Ehrman pointed out that the books from the
library were permitted to be kept overnight in one's cell and that
the "actual copying of a letter of this length would not require a
full evening's work" ("Response," 159, n. 8).

39   Robert Curzon, Jr., *Ancient Monasteries of the East or Visits to
Monasteries in the Levant* (1849; repr. Piscataway, NJ: Gorgias,
2001), 178.

40   See Geoffrey Ashall Glaister, ed., *Encyclopedia of the Book* (New
Castle, Del.: Oak Knoll, 1996), 51.

41   The literary output of Mar Saba in the seventeenth and eighteenth centuries does not support the presence of this book during those centuries. According to Siméon Vailhé's study of the
writers of Mar Saba, they showed little interest in the ante-
Nicene patristic writers and nothing specific for Ignatius and
Clement ("Les écrivains de Mar-Saba," *Échos d'Orient* 2 [1898]:
1–11 and 33–47, especially at 46).

42 Cf. Winsome Munro, "Women Disciples: Light from Secret Mark," *JFSR* 8 (2001): 48, n. 5: "As it is, Smith's scholarly standing and integrity, along with his detailed analysis of the letter (*Secret Gospel* 67–85), seem to have won the day."

43 The portion in ellipses reads: "Besides these there were some twenty distinct manuscripts and two large folders full of scraps which I did not have time to study. My notes on the collection have been printed in an article, ' Ἑλληνικά χειρόγραφα ἐν τῇ Μονῇ τοῦ ἁγίου Σάββα,' translated by Archimandrite Constantine Michaelides, in the periodical of the Patriarchate of Jerusalem, *Νέα Σιών* 52 (1960) 110ff., 245ff. To this article readers must be referred for a description of the manuscript material as a whole."

44 Smith, " Ἑλληνικά," 111; note also the present tense verb in " Ἐκτὸς τῶν προμνησθέντων χειρογράφων ὑπαρχουσιν εἰς τὴν βιβλιοθήκεν, [Apart from the aforementioned manuscripts present in the library]" (256).

45 Another example is: "In sum, it is false that I held, before discovering the new text, the theory to which it led me" (Smith, "Authenticity," 196). Smith's claim of "discovering the new text" is embedded within a clause he explicitly labeled "false."

46 Smith, "Authenticity," 196.

47 Smith, "Authenticity," 196.

48 Smith, "Authenticity," 197 (footnote omitted). The labeling of Quesnell's "insinuation" as "preposterous" in the next sentence is an attack on the soundness of Quesnell's logic, not its truth. Since Quesnell denied making that insinuation ("A Reply to Morton Smith," 200), the logic behind a charge not actually made would be insufficient as a matter of course.

49 At the time of Smith's non-denial, the public was being gripped by similar evasions in the Watergate scandal; see Carl Bernstein and Bob Woodward, *All the President's Men* (1974; repr. 2d ed., New York: Touchstone, 1994), 92.

50 Smith, "Monasteries," 172–77.

51 Smith, "Monasteries," 173 and Smith, " Ἑλληνικά," 118–19. The fragmentary manuscript was published as Morton Smith, "New Fragments of Scholia on Sophocles' *Ajax*," *GRBS* 3 (1960): 40–42.

116   NOTES TO PP. 42–45

52 Smith, "Monasteries," 175 and Smith, " Ἑλληνικά," 119–21.
53 Smith, " Ἑλληνικά," 119–20. The Greek text of the catalog reads:
    Τὸ παρὸν βιβλίον περιλαμβάνεται εἰς τὸν ἡμέτερον κατάλογον
    οὐχὶ μόνον ὡς ὑπόδειγμα συμπεπληρωμένων χειρογράφων
    (ἐκ τῶν ὁποίων ἡ βιβιοθήκη περιέχει πλεῖστα ὅσα), ἀλλ᾽ ἐπίσης
    διότι τοῦτο εἶναι ἰδιαιτέρως πλούσιον εἰς σημειώσεις ὑπὸ
    προηγουμένων κατόχων ἢ χρησιμοποιησάντων τοῦτο· f. 1r., Μ.
    Μαδιότης (χειρόγραφον ΧΧ αἰῶνος). Ὁ μοναχὸς Διονύσιος,
    ᾽Αρχιμανδρίτης, (χειρόγραφον ΧΙΧ αἰῶνος) · ....᾽Ανοβος μον–
    αχὸς τοῦ Παναγίου Τάφου (ΧVΙΙΙ αἰῶνος;). ... "
54 J. T. Pring, ed., *The Pocket Oxford Greek Dictionary* (Oxford:
    Oxford University Press, 1995), 110: "μαδώ *v.i.* & *i.* pluck,
    moult, shed hair, leaves, *etc.*; fall, come out (*of hair, leaves, etc.*);
    (*fam.*) pluck, swindle." An analogous semantic development can
    be seen in the English verb "to fleece."
55 Knox, "A New Gospel Ascribed to Mark," (a photograph of
    Smith is on page 17). Fitzmyer's observation about Smith's bald-
    ness, which had been questioned for its relevance (e.g. Eyer,
    "Strange Case of the Secret Gospel According to Mark"), takes
    on an entirely new significance in light of this pseudonym.
56 Quesnell, "Mar Saba Clementine," 51, n. 8.
57 Specifically, eight in Cephalonia, three in Dimistana, seven in
    Skiathos, and one in Yannina (Smith, "Σύμμεικτα," at 380–93).
58 Tasos Gritsopoulos, "Κατάλογος τῶν χειρογράφων κωδίκων τῆς
    βιβλιοθήκης τῆς Σχολῆς Δημητσάνης" ["A Catalog of Codex
    Manuscripts of the Library of the School of Dimistana"],
    ᾽Επετερὶς ᾽Εταιρείας Βυζαντινῶν Σπουπῶν [*Journal of the Society
    for Byzantine Studies*] 22 (1952): 183–226 and 24 (1954):
    230–74.
59 "Καλλίνικος Γ᾽," n.p. [cited 10 May 2005]. http://www.ec-patr
    .gr/gr/list/kallinikosgeikones.htm: "Γεννήθηκε στὴ Ζαγορά τοῦ
    Πηλίου τὸ 1713." Zagora is in Thessaly on the Greek mainland.
    The web page is accessible from the home page of the
    Ecumenical Patriarchate at http://www.ec-patr.gr/ by following
    the link to the Modern Greek pages, then accessing the List of
    Patriarchs (ΚΑΤΑΛΟΓΟΣ ΠΑΤΡΙΑΕΧΩΝ).
60 Calder, "Morton Smith†," 383.
61 Calder, "Morton Smith†," 383.

62 Maria Amaritou, *Τὸ γράψιμο καὶ ἡ ἀγωγή* (Athens, 1935); call number Z43.A5 1935 in the Morton Smith Collection of the Library of the Jewish Theological Seminary. The book does not contain signs of ownership prior to Smith's. The section on eighteenth-century handwriting starts on p. 256 and various ligatures are shown on p. 265.

63 Otto Stählin, ed., *Clemens Alexandrinus* (GCS; Leipzig: Hinrichs, 1905); call number BR60.G7C6 1905 in the Morton Smith Collection of the Library of the Jewish Theological Seminary.

64 Koppenhaver, *Attorney's Guide to Document Examination*, 141–42.

65 In Στρωματεὺς, πρεσβύτερος, ἄριστος, τῇ, κατὰ, and Χριστὸν. Only συντάττων exhibits a two-stroke short *tau*.

Chapter 4

1 Most notably, Crossan, *Four Other Gospels*, 68, who responsibly prefaced his analysis with this italicized disclaimer: "*The authenticity of a text can only be established by the consensus of experts who have studied the original document under scientifically appropriate circumstances.*"

2 Hedrick, "Stalemate," 141: "Clementine scholars, have, in the main, accepted the authenticity of Clement's letter (it is included among the standard texts of Clement in a 1980 German publication)."

3 Ursula Treu, "Vorwort zur zweiten Auflage," *Clemens Alexandrinus* 4.1 (GCS 39.1; Berlin: Akademie-Verlag, 1980), viii.

4 Smith, "Score," 452.

5 Eric Osborn, "Clement of Alexandria: A Review of Research, 1958–1982," *SecCent* 3 (1983): 225, concluding that "Clement's style added to a failure to comprehend Clement's ideas implies a forgery."

6 E.g., Annewies van den Hoek, "Techniques of Quotation in Clement of Alexandria: A View of Ancient Literary Working Methods," *VC* 50 (1996): 226.

7 E.g., Harold Somers and Fiona Tweedie, "Authorship Attribution and Pastiche," *Computers and the Humanities* 37 (2003): 407–29, at 412. The authors note that this assumption is problematic, however, when applied to "clever pastiches" (423).

8   A. H. Criddle, "On the Mar Saba Letter Attributed to Clement of Alexandria," *JECS* 3 (1995): 215–20.

9   Criddle, "On the Mar Saba Letter," 217.

10   Criddle, "On the Mar Saba Letter," 218.

11   The seven new *hapax legomena* are ἀναδέστατος, ἀπέρατος, ἀπόγραφον, ἀπροφυλάκτως, μηχανάω (act.), προσπορεύομαι, and φθονερῶς, while the fifteen eliminated *hapax legomena* are ἀνδραποδώδης, ἀσφαλῶς, ἐνσώματος, ἐξαγγέλλω, ἐξαντλέω, ἑπτάκις, ἐριχώ, ἱεροφαντικός, καταψεύδομαι, μωρία, πνευματι–κώτερος, προσεπάγω, Σατανᾶς, στενός, and χρησιμώτατος.

12   Specifically, Criddle treated active and middle forms of the same verb as the same word, and did not count unique vocabulary in the parts of Mark that Clement quoted ("On the Mar Saba Letter," 217).

13   To determine whether the discrepancy was statistically significant, Criddle performed a *chi*-square test on the observed number of new and old *hapax legomena* in *Theodore* as compared with the expected number of new and old *hapax legomena* for a similarly sized sample from recognized Clementine works ("On the Mar Saba Letter," 218). Criddle also performed the test with Smith's definition, and the difference was more statistically significant.

     Scott G. Brown's attempt to criticize Criddle's analysis for "being based on an exceptionally small excerpt" (*Mark's Other Gospel*, 56) flounders on a couple of misconceptions. First, the entire point of statistical significance is to assess whether the observed differences for a test statistic are unexpected for its sample size. Second, the *chi*-square test Criddle used is employed with similarly ranged numbers. See, generally, Harry Frank Althoen and Steven C. Althoen, *Statistics: Concepts and Applications* (Cambridge: Cambridge University Press, 1994), 326–78 (hypothesis testing) and 616–89 (Pearson's *chi*-square).

14   Criddle, "On the Mar Saba Letter," 216.

15   A point brought up by Andrew Criddle, "Secret Mark—Further Comments." http://www-user.uni-bremen.de/~wie/Secret/Criddle -Feb99.html. See also Charles E. Murgia as quoted by Irene Lawrence, recorder, "Minutes of the Colloquy of 7 December

1975," in *Longer Mark: Forgery, Interpolation, or Old Tradition?* (edited by W. Wuellner; Protocol of the Eighteenth Colloquy; Berkeley, Calif.: Center for Hermeneutical Studies, 1976), 62: "The style of a letter should be different from the style of generically different writing, so if we prove this style the same as in the *Stromateis*, we have proved too much." The stability of an author's style is also dependent on the author's age. If the least problematic time in Clement's life for writing *Theodore* is after his exile from Alexandria and after his surviving works were composed, then even greater stylistic differences should be apparent.

16 Cf. Athanasios Papadopoulos-Kerameus,ʹΙεροσολυμιτικη Βιβλιο–θήκη (1894; Brussels: Culture & Civilisation, 1963), 2:851, having entries only for Clement I of Rome, Clement III of Rome, Clement the poet, Clement the bishop of Ancyra, Clement the hieromonk of the Holy Sepulcher (1617–1619), and Clement the hieromonk (1769).

17 Many of Clement's works have been lost, including the eight-book commentary *Hypotyposeis*. Eusebius lists four other works of Clement that have not survived: Περὶ τοῦ πάσχα, Περὶ νηστείας, Περὶ καταλαλιᾶς, and Κανὼν ἐκκλησιαστικὸς ἢ πρὸς τοὺς Ἰουδαίζοντας (from Andrew J. Carriker, *The Library of Eusebius of Caesarea* [Leiden: Brill, 2003], 197–98).

18 Indeed, Andrew Criddle (pers. comm., Jan. 2004) has discovered commonalities between *Theodore* and the *Philosophumena* in the mystery religion terminology and concepts in Hippolytus's description of the Naassenes. Since the *Philosophumena* was rediscovered only in 1841, Criddle concluded that these commonalities would seem to exclude an eighteenth-century forgery. These commonalities do not exclude Smith, however.

19 According to Paul Keyser, review of Leonard Brandwood, *The Chronology of Plato's Dialogues*, BMCR 3.1.12 (1992). http://ccat.sas.upenn.edu/bmcr/1992/03.01.12.html. Generally credited to F. E. D. Schleiermacher, *Über den sogenannten ersten Brief des Paulos an den Timotheos* (Berlin: 1807), 27–76; repr. *Friedrich Schleiermacher's sämtliche Werke* 1.2 (Berlin: 1836), 221–320, at 233–54.

20 Quesnell, "Mar Saba Clementine," 55.

21 Pace Herbert Musurillo, "Morton Smith's Secret Gospel," *Thought* 48 (1973): 327–31, who raises the possibility of an eighteenth-century forgery.

22 Charles E. Murgia, "Secret Mark: Real or Fake?" in *Longer Mark: Forgery, Interpolation, or Old Tradition?* (ed. W. Wuellner; Protocol of the Eighteenth Colloquy; Berkeley, Calif.: Center for Hermeneutical Studies, 1976), 35–40.

23 Murgia's example of a genuine *sphragis* is Virgil's practice of ending his works with an imitation of the first line of one of his previous works ("Secret Mark," 36). One use of *sphragis* is exemplified by Theognis of Megara, *Elegiae* 1.19–20: Κύρνε, σοφιζομένωι μὲν ἐμοὶ σφρηγὶς ἐπικείσθω τοῖσδ᾽ ἔπεσιν ("Cyrnus, let a seal I devise be laid upon these words)" (D. Young, ed., *Theognis* [2d ed.; Leipzig: Teubner, 1971]).

24 This is one reason why a verifiable provenance is a critical safeguard against contemporary falsifications.

25 Murgia, "Secret Mark," 37.

26 Murgia, "Secret Mark," 38.

27 Smith, "Score," 451.

28 E.g., John L. White, *Light from Ancient Letters* (Philadelphia: Fortress, 1986), 214–16.

29 White, *Light from Ancient Letters*, 215. See also Harry Y. Gamble, *Books and Readers in the Earlier Church: A History of Early Christian Texts* (New Haven: Yale University Press, 1995), 96.

30 See generally, Bauckham, "Pseudo-Apostolic Letters," 475.

31 Patricia A. Rosenmeyer, *Ancient Epistolary Fictions: The Letter in Greek Literature* (Cambridge: Cambridge University Press, 2001), 208.

32 Rosenmeyer, *Ancient Epistolary Fictions*, 209.

33 Attila Jakab, "Une lettre «perdue» de Clément d'Alexandrie? (Morton Smith et l'«Évangile secret» de Marc)," *Apocrypha* 10 (1999): 7–15, at 13. Jakab also found it troubling that Clement showed more confidence in describing the Carpocratians in *Theodore* than in his acknowledged works (13–14). Also problematic for Jakab was that *Theodore*'s tale of Mark's arrival implied that Christianity had already been present in Alexandria contrary to Eusebius and that Mark died of natural causes contrary to Coptic tradition (14–15).

34 William L. Petersen, "The Genesis of the Gospels" in *New Testament Textual Criticism and Exegesis: Festschrift J. Delobel* (ed. A. Denaux; BETL 161; Leuven: Leuven University Press, 2002), 33–65, esp. 37–39. For studies of the text of Clement's quotations, see also M. Mees, *Die Zitate aus dem Neuen Testament bei Clemens von Alexandrien* (QVC 2; Bari: Instituto di Letteratura Cristiana Antica, 1970); P. Mordaunt Barnard, *Clement of Alexandria's Biblical Text* (TS 5.5; Cambridge: Cambridge University Press, 1899). Reuben J. Swanson, *New Testament Greek Manuscripts: Mark* (Sheffield: Sheffield Academic Press, 1995) included Clement's text in his horizontal-line edition.

35 That is, ὅπου εἰσέτι νῦν ἀσφαλῶς εὖ μάλα τηρεῖται ("where it even yet is most carefully guarded"; *Theod.* II.1). Scott G. Brown tried to mute the force of this secrecy motif in *Theodore* by arguing that this merely means "most carefully preserved," "most perfectly respected," or even "unerringly appropriated" ("The More Spiritual Gospel," 178–83), but, aside from such metaphorical uses of τηρέω being found with abstract objects (e.g. keeping laws or preserving dignity), Brown's toned-down proposal makes little contextual sense of why Carpocrates would have needed to enslave a presbyter to obtain the text if it had not been carefully guarded but merely respected.

36 Actually, the presence of homosexual activity among the Carpocratians is not evident in Clement's descriptions of them in his acknowledged works. For example, in *Stromata* 3, Clement describes their practice of sharing their wives (A. Criddle, pers. comm.).

37 Cf. Smith, "Comments," 26, supposing a source with "Johannine traits" behind Mark's healing of the paralytic.

38 *Quis div.* 4.4–10.

39 For example, the early second-century Papias as quoted in Eusebius, *Hist. eccl.* 3.39.15: Μάρκος μὲν ἑρμηνευτὴς Πέτρου γενόμενος, ὅσα ἐμνημόνευσεν, ἀκριβῶς ἔγραψεν, οὐ μέντοι τάξει τὰ ὑπὸ τοῦ κυρίου ἢ λεχθέντα ἢ πραχθέντα ("Mark, who had indeed been Peter's interpreter, accurately wrote as much as he remembered, yet not in order, about what was either said or done by the Lord").

40 Eusebius, *Hist. eccl.* 6.14.6: τοὺς παρόντας, πολλοὺς ὄντας, παρακαλέσαι τὸν Μάρκον, ὡς ἃ ἀκολουθήσαντα αὐτῷ πόρρωθεν καὶ μεμνημένον τῶν λεχθέντων, ἀναγράψαι τὰ εἰρημένα. *Theodore* also differs from Clement's etiology in *Hypotyposeis* in other details. For example, Stephen C. Carlson, "Clement of Alexandria on the 'Order' of the Gospels," *NTS* 47 (2001): 118–25, has shown that Clement employed the verb προγράφω in a locative, not chronological sense, to mean that Matthew and Luke, unlike Mark, were openly published. However, with respect to its usage in *Hypotyposeis*, *Theodore*'s use of the same verb for the canonical gospel of Mark (προγεγραμμέναις in I.24) is either lexically incongruous if it means "previously written" or substantively contradictory if it means "openly published."

41 Cf. Murgia, "Secret Mark," 37: " 'An interpolator would have avoided the contradiction,' critics are meant to and do say. A really clever interpolator knows enough to put one in."

42 Smith's argument rests on a false dichotomy between *Theodore* and the surviving works of Clement. On the one hand, some of Clement's surviving works can hardly be characterized as "published works." In particular, the *Excerpta of Theodotus* by Clement is a set of notes for a future project, not a published work. On the other hand, if the apparent transmission of *Theodore* is to be believed, it must have been published in a letter collection without censorship, probably by Clement himself, or, if posthumously published, left among his papers as Smith had argued for the letters of Isidore of Pelusium. Smith, "Manuscript Tradition," 208.

43 John Ferguson, *Clement of Alexandria: Stromateis Books 1–3* (FC 85; Washington, DC: Catholic University of America Free Press, 1991), 52–53 (footnotes to Titus 1:10 and Matthew 5:13 omitted).

44 This is probably not what Jesus meant by the saying, however. An interpretation that probably makes the best sense in first-century Judea and Galilee is that the sodium chloride in the salt compositions obtained from the Dead Sea can be slowly leached out by moisture in the air, leaving less palatable minerals (Eugene P. Deatrick, "Salt, Soil, Savior," *BA* 25 [1962]: 41–48).

45 See generally, Garrett Laidlaw Eskew, *Salt: The Fifth Element* (Chicago: Ferguson, 1948), 152–59.

46 W. D. Davies and Dale C. Allison, Jr., *Matthew* (3 vols.; ICC; Edinburgh, T&T Clark, 1988) argue, "But the question about salt . . . should be explained by the indisputable fact that salt can be so mixed with impurities as to become useless (cf. Pliny, Nat. hist. 31.82)" (1:473). This is apparently in reference to Pliny's text at *Nat. hist.* 31.82: *in Chaonia excocunt aquam ex fonte refrigerandoque salem facient inertum nec candidum* ("In Chaonia there is a spring, from which they boil water, and on cooling obtain a salt that is insipid and not white"; trans. W. H. S. Jones). Whether the Chaonian salt is insipid due to being mixed with impurities, however, is a modern analysis; Pliny is silent on the reason and the passage does not support intentional adulteration of salt.

47 A. E. R. Boak, "An Ordinance of the Salt Merchants," *AJP* 58 (1937): 210–19, quotation coming from P. Mich. Inv. 657 (47 CE), lines 24–26.

48 Eskew, *Salt*, 172–73. The potassium iodide was chemically unstable, but scientists were eventually able to prevent this with application of another chemical (dextrose), which allowed for smaller amounts of potassium iodide (KI) to be used, so that, apart from gourmands, people now are not usually able to distinguish iodized salt from non-iodized salt in blind-taste trials. See, e.g., Clive E. West, et al., "Effect of Iodized Salt on the Colour and Taste of Food," UNICEF No. PD/95/009 (June 1995). http://www.micronutrient.org/Salt_CD/4.0_useful/4.1_fulltext/pdfs/4.1.4.pdf.

49 Mary Virginia Orna, et al., "Applications of Infrared Microspectroscopy to Art Historical Questions about Medieval Manuscripts," *Archaeological Chemistry* 4 (1988): 270–88. The catalog number of Archaic Mark at the University of Chicago is MS 972; among New Testament textual critics, it is known as Gregory-Aland 2427 (see Kurt Aland, *Kurzgefaßte Liste der griechischen Hanschriften des neuen Testaments* [ANT 1; 2d. ed.; Berlin: Walter de Gruyter, 1994], 187). Since illuminations have been added to or retouched in old manuscripts to increase their sales price, the modernity of the pigment discovered in the

illuminations does not completely resolve whether *Archaic Mark*'s unusual text is medieval or modern.

50 Adapted from Lancelot C. L. Brenton, *The Septuagint with Apocrypha: Greek and English* (London: Bagster, 1851; repr. Peabody, Mass.: Hendrickson, 1992), 938, which reads: "Every man has completely lost understanding; . . . for they have cast false gods, there is no breath in them." Brenton's translation is based on a variant reading (ἐματαιώθη for ἐμωράνθη) and he rendered ψευδῆ more explicitly as "false *gods*" (italics original indicating an added word).

51 Brenton, *Septuagint with Apocrypha*, 938 (italics removed).

52 Smith, "Authenticity," 197.

53 Smith, "Authenticity," 197, n. 7.

54 Smith, "Image of God," 482, n. 2 = *Studies*, ed. Cohen, 1:124, n. 33.

Chapter 5

1 Recent defenders of *Secret Mark*'s antiquity include Scott G. Brown, "The More Spiritual Gospel" and *Mark's Other Gospel*, and John Dart, *Decoding Mark* (Harrisburg: Trinity, 2003). Brown argued that *Secret Mark* was an expanded edition written by the same author who composed the canonical Mark, and Brown based his finding that the fragments of *Secret Mark* form new intercalations with other parts of Mark, a noticeable aspect of Mark's style (298–305). However, the criteria Brown used are too lenient and cannot distinguish genuine cases of intercalation and *inclusio* from the kind of intertextual references that forgers ordinarily insert to lend an air of legitimacy to their handiwork. Dart's case has been criticized because it depends on a conjectural emendation to the text of Mark; see Lincoln H. Blumell, review of John Dart, *Decoding Mark*, *Review of Biblical Literature* [http://www.bookreviews.org] (2004) and Mark Schuler, *Decoding Mark*, *Review of Biblical Literature* [http://www.bookreviews.org] (2004).

2 Ehrman, *Lost Christianities*, 81 (subtitle "The Question of Forgery" omitted).

3 Raymond E. Brown, "The Relation of the 'Secret Gospel of Mark' to the Fourth Gospel," *CBQ* 36 (1974): 466–85, suggested

that John 1:39, καὶ παρ᾽ αὐτῷ ἔμειναν τὴν ἡμέραν ἐκείνην ("and they spent that day with him") is a "particularly good parallel" (479). However, the preposition, word order, the time period, and the number of the verb are all different. Thus, Brown's proposed parallel in another gospel actually shows how different this clause is.

4 This analysis has been performed by searching for texts with the word νύκτα "night" within one line of the preposition σύν "with" and scrutinizing all 64 hits one by one. Since it is not uncommon for non-native speakers to use the wrong preposition, a search of the TLG database was also performed using the preposition μετά ("with"), which yielded only two instances (Herm. Sim. 11 [88].6; Hippolytus [Narr. de virg. Corinth.] 277). Both of these occurred in contexts in which no sexual activity took place.

5 E.g., Smith, Tannaitic Parallels to the Gospels, xi: "In translation I have often preferred idiomatic English to word-for-word accuracy." See also Morton Smith, "Notes on Goodspeed's 'Problems of New Testament Translation,' " JBL 64 (1945): 501–14, at 513: "But it seems desirable to translate an idiom by an equivalent idiom."

6 E.g., Helmut Koester, "The Secret Gospel of Mark," in The Complete Gospels (ed. Robert J. Miller; Sonoma, Calif.: Polebridge, 1994), 411.

7 R. W. Holder, ed., A Dictionary of Euphemisms (Oxford: Oxford University Press, 1995), 348.

8 Theodore M. Bernstein, The Careful Writer: A Modern Guide to English Usage (1965; repr., New York: Free Press, 1995), 171, s.v. euphemism.

9 Smith rejected this possibility with a rather weak argument from silence: "However Clement does not explicitly say that the additional material was sexually offensive, and he would hardly have missed the chance to say so if it had been" (Clement 185). Since Theodore breaks off shortly afterwards in mid-sentence, how could Smith know "that Clement missed the chance to say so"?

10 Holder, Dictionary of Euphemisms, vii.

11 John Ayto, ed., Bloomsbury Dictionary of Euphemisms (rev. ed.; London: Bloomsbury, 2000), 69–70.

12 Further assistance to the modern reader comes from *Theodore's* opening denunciation of the Carpocratians that quoted Jude, a mostly neglected New Testament text used in the twentieth-century to condemn homosexuality.

13 E.g., Michel Foucault, *The History of Sexuality* (trans. Robert Hurley; New York: Random House, 1978; repr. 1990), 43: "Westphal's famous article of 1870 on 'contrary sexual sensa-tions' can stand as its birth. . . . The sodomite had been a tempo-rary aberration; the homosexual was a species." See also Jonathan Ned Katz, *The Invention of Heterosexuality* (New York: Dutton, 1995).

14 E.g., David M. Halperin, *One Hundred Years of Homosexuality* (New York: Routledge, 1990).

15 See Halperin, *One Hundred Years of Homosexuality*, 33: "Even the relevant features of a sexual object in classical Athens were not so much determined by a physical typology of the sexes as by the social articulation of power."

16 καὶ τὸ τῆς ἡλικίας [ἀλλήλοις] ἀνύποπτον ἦν (*Ephesiaca* 3.2.4). I owe this example to Halperin, *One Hundred Years of Homosexu-ality*, 169, n. 9.

17 Marvin Meyer, *Secret Gospels: Essays on Thomas and the Secret Gospel of Mark* (Harrisburg: Trinity, 2003). Diogenes assigned the first twenty years for a παῖς, while Philo subdivided the ranges as between seven and thirteen for a παῖς, and between fourteen and twenty for a μειράκιον. Also Brown, *Mark's Other Gospel*, 239, n. 3: "The Greek term here translated 'young man' (neaniskos) normally refers to a male in his twenties."

18 *Lawrence v. Texas*, 539 US 558 (2003) (Kennedy, J.). See also William N. Eskridge, Jr., "Hardwick and Historiography," *University of Illinois Law Review* 1999 (1999): 631–97.

19 John Howard, "The Library, the Park, and the Pervert: Public Space and Homosexual Encounter in Post-World War II Atlanta," in *Carryin' On in the Lesbian and Gay South* (ed. John Howard; New York: New York University Press, 1997), 108.

20 John D'Emilio and Estelle B. Freedman, *Intimate Matters: A History of Sexuality in America* (New York: Harper & Row, 1988), 293–94.

21 N.Y. Penal Law § 722(8), later recodified at N.Y. Code §240.35(3). For determining guilt or innocence, courts ruled that it is "immaterial if the object of the solicitation is never consummated." *People v. McCormack*, 9 Misc.2d 745, 169 N.Y.S.2d 139 (1957).

22 *People v. Uplinger*, 58 N.Y.2d 936, 460 N.Y.S.2d 574, 447 N.E.2d 62, cert. dismissed as improvidently granted, 467 U.S. 246, 104 S.Ct. 2332, 81 L.E.2d 201 (1983). The ordinance was struck down, because the highest court of New York had, just three years earlier, legalized the ordinance's predicate act under the New York state constitution in *People v. Onofre*, 51 N.Y.2d 476, 434 N.Y.S.2d 947, 415 N.E.2d 936, cert. denied, 451 U.S. 987, 101 S.Ct. 2323, 68 L.E.2d 845 (1980).

23 Derrick Sherwin Bailey, *Homosexuality and the Western Cultural Tradition* (London: Longmans, Green, 1955): 66–68.

24 Louis Crompton, *Byron and Greek Love: Homophobia in 19th-Century England* (Berkeley: University of California, 1985), 281–82, discussing Bentham's letter of November 28, 1817, which credited the identification to a comment in the *Monthly Magazine* for September 1811. Instead of making the criminal connection, Bentham emphasized the stripling's devotion to Jesus to a degree that exceeded that of the disciples and concluded from this that Jesus lacked "reprobation towards the mode of sexuality in question."

25 The portion in ellipses reads: "And Paul himself wrote I Cor. 2.1-6 'And I, coming to you, brethren, came not proclaiming the testimony of God in lofty words or wisdom . . . that your faith might not be in the wisdom of men, but in the power of God. But we speak the wisdom among the perfect, and a wisdom not of this age . . . but we speak the wisdom of God in a mystery.'" Smith, *Tannaitic Parallels to the Gospels*, 156. This passage too has a parallel in *Theodore*: ἐν τοῖς τελείος ("among the perfect") in 1 Cor. 2:6 and εἰς τὴν τῶν τελειουμένων χρῆσιν ("for the use of those who were being perfected") in *Theod.* I.22.

26 Smith, *Tannaitic Parallels to the Gospels*, 155–56.

27 Smith, "Image of God," 507 = *Studies*, ed. Cohen, 1:145, nn. 151 and 152.

Chapter 6

1 Brown, *Mark's Other Gospel*, 13.

2 Smith, "Notes on Goodspeed's," 501–14. For example, Smith preferred "So you say" over Goodspeed's "Yes" for Σὺ λέγεις at Matthew 27:11 because it better captures the original's ambiguity (506–9). Similarly, Smith preferred "comprehend" or "master" for καταλαβάνω in John 1:5 over Goodspeed's "put out" (510–11). Neither Brown's dissertation nor his book enumerated this article in their bibliographies.

3 Cohen, "In Memoriam Morton Smith," 2:283. Cf. William M. Calder, III, "SMITH, Morton," in *Biographical Dictionary of North American Classicsts* (ed. Ward W. Briggs, Jr.; Westport, Conn.: Greenwood, 1994), 600: "He learned Hebrew in a year and obtained a Sheldon Fellowship for study at the Hebrew University of Jerusalem." It is also telling that none of the real or imagined faults that Jacob Neusner leveled at Smith after his death in *Are There Really Tannaitic Parallels to the Gospels? A Refutation of Morton Smith* (SFSHJ 80; Atlanta: Scholars, 1993) included Smith's facility in Greek. For a brief itemization of the faults, see Shaye J. D. Cohen, "Are There Tannaitic Parallels to the Gospels?" *JAOS* 116 (1996): 85–89, at 85.

4 Lawrence, "Minutes," 60. Murgia's statement about Smith's sense of humor, "I detect no attempt at humor in the book," actually betrays his unfamiliarity with Smith. Cf. Cohen, "In Memoriam Morton Smith," 2:279: "Morton Smith (1915–1991) was a great scholar, blessed with extraordinary acuity, mordant wit, and expansive range."

5 A less likely possibility is that Murgia's slight was an attempt to provoke a confession from the hoaxer by attacking his ego. However, Smith was not present when Murgia made the comment, and, in any case, it did not work.

6 Smith, "Score," 450. The "no one else" was Quesnell.

7 Brown, *Mark's Other Gospel*, 38. Cf. Brown, "The More Spiritual Gospel," 128: "It is also worth noting that Smith's work on longer Mark constitutes his only substantial study in the area of Patristics. He otherwise showed very little aptitude to study second-century church fathers."

8 Smith, "Image of God," 482, n. 2; 501, n. 3; 507, n. 5; and 511,

n. 5. These are reprinted in *Studies*, ed. Cohen 1:124, n. 33; 1:139, n. 110; 1:145, n. 152; and 1:148, n. 174.

9   Smith's familiarity with Hippolytus is why the commonalities between *Theodore* and the *Philosophumena* that Andrew Criddle has discovered (see above ch. 4, n. 18) cannot exclude Smith as the author of *Theodore*.

10 Specifically, the manuscript material for Smith's *Life of Isidore* was deposited in Brown University Library where Smith worked from 1950–1955 (Smith, "Unpublished Life," 431), and Smith had become interested in the account of the Essenes in Hippolytus's *Philosophumena* by his colleagues at Drew, where he worked from 1955–1957 (Smith, "Description," 273).

11 Brown, *Mark's Other Gospel*, 73.

12 Smith, "Σύμμεικτα," 383.

13 See *Studies*, ed. Cohen, 2:257–78.

14 Brown also seems unaware of the materials in the Morton Smith Collection pertinent to this issue.

15 Brown, "The More Spiritual Gospel," 133.

16 Brown, "The More Spiritual Gospel," 133, n. 200.

17 Morton Smith, "In Quest of Jesus," *New York Review of Books* 25, no. 20, December 21, 1978.

18 Calder, "SMITH, Morton," 600–602, at 602: "The vast *Nachlaß* of personal and scholarly correspondence was destroyed by Smith's literary executor, David Smith, in accord with his wishes in 1991."

19 Love, *Attributing Authorship*, 185.

20 Noticed by Quesnell, "Mar Saba Clementine," 66: "Who is 'the one who knows'? What does he know?"

21 Calder, "Morton Smith†," 383.

22 Calder, "Morton Smith†," 384.

23 Grafton, *Forgers and Critics*, 40–41 (footnote omitted).

24 Quesnell, "Mar Saba Clementine," 58–60; Smith, "Authenticity," 198. Quesnell's raising of this topic is not particularly clear, however; at times he seems to be merely wondering why Smith's historical sketch was so irrelevant to *Secret Mark*.

25 This continues to trap even supporters of *Secret Mark*. See, e.g., Brown, *Mark's Other Gospel*, 49–54.

26 Smith, "Comments on Taylor's Commentary," 26.

27 Smith, "Comments on Taylor's Commentary," 63.

28 Taylor, *The Gospel According to St. Mark*, 195: "Jesus by no means believed that sin was the sole cause of affliction and calamity (cf. Jn. ix. 2, Lk. xiii. 1-5), but He could not fail to observe how closely mental, spiritual, and physical conditions are connected, in this respect anticipating the conclusions of modern psychotherapy regarding hysterical forms of paralysis."

29 Taylor, *The Gospel According to St. Mark*, 286.

30 Smith, "Comments on Taylor's Commentary," 36.

31 Smith, "Comments on Taylor's Commentary," 26.

32 Smith, "Comments on Taylor's Commentary," 32.

33 Smith, "Comments on Taylor's Commentary," 63–64.

34 A. Baumgarten, "Smith, Morton (1915–91)," in *Dictionary of Biblical Interpretation: K–Z* (Nashville: Abington, 1999), 477.

35 Calder, "Morton Smith†," 382.

36 Cohen, "In Memoriam Morton Smith," 2:285.

37 See, e.g., Howard, "The Library, the Park, and the Pervert," 108: "Specifically, I will show that the tenets of Protestant Christianity suffused institutional responses to a growing homosexual threat in postwar Atlanta, even as the targets of such surveillance—gay men caught in the act, in public spaces—likewise shared deep personal ties to an evangelical tradition."

38 Calder, "Morton Smith†," 382.

39 Calder, "Morton Smith†," 384.

40 Morton Smith, "The Present State of Old Testament Studies," *JBL* 88 (1969): 19–35 at 23; repr. in *Studies*, ed. Cohen, 1:37–54 at 1:41.

Chapter 7

1 Edgar Goodspeed, *Modern Apocrypha* (Boston: Beacon, 1956), 3–14.

2 Harold Love, *Attributing Authorship: An Introduction* (Cambridge: Cambridge University Press, 2002), 184.

3 E.g., J. S. Weimer, *The Piltdown Forgery* (1955; 2d ed.; Oxford: Oxford University Press, 2004).

4 E.g., André Lemaire, "Burial Box of James the Brother of Jesus," *BAR* 28.6 (2002): 24–33.

5 Ehrman, "Response," 159.

Works Cited

Achtemeier, Paul J. Reviews of *Clement of Alexandria* and *The Secret Gospel, JBL* 93 (1974): 625–28.

Akenson, Donald Harman. *Saint Saul: A Skeleton Key to the Historical Jesus.* Oxford: Oxford University Press, 2000.

———. *Surpassing Wonder: The Invention of the Bible and the Talmuds.* Chicago: University of Chicago Press, 1998.

Aland, Kurt. *Kurzgefaßte Liste der griechischen Hanschriften des neuen Testaments.* ANT 1. 2d. ed. Berlin: Walter de Gruyter, 1994.

Alexander, Patrick H., et al., eds. *The SBL Handbook of Style: For Ancient Near Eastern, Biblical, and Early Christian Studies.* Peabody, Mass.: Hendrickson, 1999.

Althoen, Harry Frank, and Steven C. Althoen. *Statistics: Concepts and Applications.* Cambridge: Cambridge University Press, 1994.

Amaritou, Maria. Τὸ γράψιμο καὶ ἡ ἀγωγή. Athens, 1935.

Ayto, John, ed. *Bloomsbury Dictionary of Euphemisms.* Rev. ed. London: Bloomsbury, 2000.

Bagnani, Gilbert. "On Fakes and Forgeries." *Phoenix* 14 (1960): 228–44.

Bailey, Derrick Sherwin. *Homosexuality and the Western Cultural Tradition.* London: Longmans, Green, 1955.

Baldi, Philip. *The Foundation of Latin.* Trends in Linguistics Studies and Monographs 117. Berlin: Mouton de Gruyter, 1999.

Barnard, P. Mordaunt. *Clement of Alexandria's Biblical Text*. TS 5.5. Cambridge: Cambridge University Press, 1899.

Bauckham, Richard. "Pseudo-Apostolic Letters." *JBL* 107 (1988): 469–94.

Baumgarten, A. "Smith, Morton (1915–91)." Page 477 in *Dictionary of Biblical Interpretation: K–Z*. Nashville: Abington, 1999.

Bernstein Carl, and Bob Woodward. *All the President's Men*. 1974. Repr. 2d ed. New York: Touchstone, 1994.

Bernstein, Theodore M. *The Careful Writer: A Modern Guide to English Usage*. 1965. Repr. New York: Free Press, 1995.

Beskow, Per. *Strange Tales about Jesus: A Survey of Unfamiliar Gospels*. Philadelphia: Fortress, 1983.

Best, Ernest. Review of E. J. Pryke, *Redactional Style in the Marcan Gospel*. *JSNT* 4 (1979): 71–76.

Blumell, Lincoln H. Review of John Dart, *Decoding Mark*, *Review of Biblical Literature* [http://www.bookreviews.org] (2004).

Boak, A. E. R. "An Ordinance of the Salt Merchants." *AJP* 58 (1937): 210–19.

Brenton, Lancelot C. L. *The Septuagint with Apocrypha: Greek and English*. London: Bagster 1851. Repr. Peabody, Mass.: Hendrickson, 1992.

Brown, Raymond E. "The Relation of the 'Secret Gospel of Mark' to the Fourth Gospel." *CBQ* 36 (1974): 466–85.

Brown, Scott G. *Mark's Other Gospel: Rethinking Morton Smith's Controversial Discovery*. ESCJ 15. Ontario: Wilfrid Laurier University Press, 2005.

———. "The More Spiritual Gospel: Markan Literary Techniques in the Longer Gospel of Mark." Ph.D. diss., U. Toronto, 1999.

———. "On the Composition History of the Longer ('Secret') Gospel of Mark." *JBL* 122 (2003): 89–110.

Calder, III, William M. "Morton Smith†." *Gn* 64 (1992): 382–83.

———. "SMITH, Morton." In *Biographical Dictionary of North American Classicists*. Edited by Ward W. Briggs, Jr. Westport, Conn.: Greenwood, 1994.

Carlson, Stephen C. "Clement of Alexandria on the 'Order' of the Gospels," *NTS* 47 (2001): 118–25.

Carriker, Andrew J. *The Library of Eusebius of Caesarea*. Leiden: Brill, 2003.

Clark, Kenneth W. *Checklist of manuscripts in the libraries of the Greek and Armenian Patriarchates in Jerusalem, microfilmed for the Library of Congress, 1949–50, prepared under the direction of Kenneth W. Clark, director and general editor of the Jerusalem Expedition, 1949–50*. Washington, DC: Library of Congress, 1953.

Cohen, Shaye J. D. "Are There Tannaitic Parallels to the Gospels?" *JAOS* 116 (1996): 85–89.

———. "In Memoriam Morton Smith" Page 279 in *Studies in the Cult of Yahweh*. Edited by Shaye J. D. Cohen. RGRW 130. Vol. 2. Leiden: Brill, 1996.

———. "Morton Smith and Secret Mark." *Ioudaios*, July 11, 1995, n.p.

———. *Studies in the Cult of Yahweh*. RGRW 130. 2 vols. Leiden: Brill, 1996.

Coleman-Norton, Paul R. "An Amusing *Agraphon*." *CBQ* 12 (1950): 439–49.

Criddle, A. H. "On the Mar Saba Letter Attributed to Clement of Alexandria," *JECS* 3 (1995): 215–20.

———. "Secret Mark—Further Comments." http://www-user.uni-bremen.de/~wie/Secret/Criddle-Feb99.html. Accessed February 1999.

Crompton, Louis. *Byron and Greek Love: Homophobia in 19th-Century England*. Berkeley: University of California, 1985.

Crossan, John Dominic. *Four Other Gospels: Shadows on the Contours of the Canon*. New York: Harper & Row, 1985. Repr. Sonoma, Calif.: Polebridge, 1992.

Curzon, Robert, Jr. *Ancient Monasteries of the East or Visits to Monasteries in the Levant*. 1849. Repr. Piscataway, NJ: Gorgias, 2001.

Dart, John. *Decoding Mark*. Harrisburg: Trinity, 2003.

Davies, W. D., and Dale C. Allison, Jr. *Matthew*. ICC. 3 vols. Edinburgh, T&T Clark, 1988.

Deatrick, Eugene P. "Salt, Soil, Savior." *BA* 25 (1962): 41–48.

DeConick, April D. "The Original Gospel of Thomas." *VC* 56 (2002): 167–99.

D'Emilio, John, and Estelle B. Freedman. *Intimate Matters: A History of Sexuality in America*. New York: Harper & Row, 1988.

Ehrman, Bart D. *Lost Christianities: The Battles for Scripture and the Faiths We Never Knew*. Oxford: Oxford University Press, 2003.

————. "Response to Charles Hedrick's Stalemate," *JECS* 11 (2003): 159, n. 8.

Eskew, Garrett Laidlaw. *Salt: The Fifth Element*. Chicago: Ferguson, 1948.

Eskridge, William N., Jr. "Hardwick and Historiography." *University of Illinois Law Review* (1999): 631–97.

Eyer, Shawn. "The Strange Case of the Secret Gospel According to Mark: How Morton Smith's Discovery of a Lost Letter by Clement of Alexandria Scandalized Biblical Scholarship." *Alexandria: The Journal for the Western Cosmological Traditions* 3 (1995): 103–29.

Ferguson, John. *Clement of Alexandria: Stromateis Books 1–3*. FC 85. Washington, DC: Catholic University of America Free Press, 1991.

Fitzmyer, Joseph A. "How to Exploit a Secret Gospel." *America*, June 23, 1973: 570–72.

Foster, Don. *Author Unknown: On the Trail of Anonymous*. New York: Henry Holt, 2000.

Foucault, Michel. *The History of Sexuality*. Trans. Robert Hurley. New York: Random House, 1978. Repr. 1990.

Frank, Harry, and Steven C. Althoen. *Statistics: Concepts and Applications*. Cambridge: Cambridge University Press, 1994.

Gamble, Harry Y. *Books and Readers in the Earlier Church: A History of Early Christian Texts*. New Haven: Yale University Press, 1995.

Glaister, Geoffrey Ashall, ed. *Encyclopedia of the Book*. New Castle, Del.: Oak Knoll, 1996.

Goodspeed, Edgar. *Modern Apocrypha*. Boston: Beacon, 1956.

Grafton, Anthony. *Forgers and Critics: Creativity and Duplicity in Western Scholarship*. Princeton: Princeton University Press, 1990.

Grant, Robert M. "Morton Smith's Two Books." *ATR* 56 (1974): 58–65.

Gritsopoulos, Tasos. "Κατάλογος τῶν χειρογράφων κωδίκων τῆς βιβλιοθήκης τῆς Σχολῆς Δημητσάνης" ["A Catalog of Codex Manuscripts of the Library of the School of Dimistana"]. *Ἐπετερὶς Ἑταιρείας Βυζαντινῶν Σπουπῶν* [*Journal of the Society for Byzantine Studies*] 22 (1952): 183–226, 24 (1954): 230–74.

Gundry, Robert H. *Mark: A Commentary on His Apology for the Cross.* Grand Rapids: Eerdmans, 1993.

Halperin, David M. *One Hundred Years of Homosexuality.* New York: Routledge, 1990.

Hamilton, Charles. *Great Forgers and Famous Fakes: The Manuscript Forgers of America and How They Duped the Experts.* 2d. ed. Lakewood, Colo.: Glenbridge, 1996.

Haren, Michael J. "The Naked Young Man: a Historian's Hypothesis on Mark 14,51–52." *Bib* 79 (1998): 525–31.

Harnack, Adolf. *Die Pfaff'schen Irenäus-Fragmente als fälschungen Pfaffs.* TU n. f. 5.3. Leipzig: Hinrichs, 1900.

Hedrick, Charles W. "The Secret Gospel of Mark: Stalemate in the Academy." *JECS* 11 (2003): 133–45.

Hedrick, Charles W., with Nikolaos Olympiou. "Secret Mark: New Photographs, New Witnesses," *Fourth R* 13, no. 5 (2000): 3–16.

Hoek, Annewies van den. "Techniques of Quotation in Clement of Alexandria: A View of Ancient Literary Working Methods." *VC* 50 (1996): 226.

Holder, R. W., ed. *A Dictionary of Euphemisms.* Oxford: Oxford University Press, 1995.

Howard, John, ed. "The Library, the Park, and the Pervert: Public Space and Homosexual Encounter in Post-World War II Atlanta." Pages 107–31 in *Carryin' On in the Lesbian and Gay South.* New York: New York University Press, 1997.

Hunter, James H. *The Mystery of Mar Saba.* Grand Rapids: Zondervan, 1940. Repr. 1947.

Hurtado, Larry W. *Lord Jesus Christ: Devotion to Jesus in Earliest Christianity.* Grand Rapids: Eerdmans, 2003.

Jakab, Attila. "Une lettre «perdue» de Clément d'Alexandrie? (Morton Smith et l'«Évangile secret» de Marc)." *Apocrypha* 10 (1999): 7–15.

Jenkins, Philip. *Hidden Gospels: How the Search for Jesus Lost Its Way.* Oxford: Oxford University Press, 2001.

Katz, Jonathan Ned. *The Invention of Heterosexuality.* New York: Dutton, 1995.

Keyser, Paul. Review of Leonard Brandwood, *The Chronology of Plato's Dialogues.* BMCR 3.1.12 (1992).

Knox, Sanka. "A New Gospel Ascribed to Mark." *The New York Times,* December 30, 1960.

———. "Expert Disputes 'Secret Gospel.' " *The New York Times,* December 31, 1960.

Koester, Helmut. *Ancient Christian Gospels: Their History and Development.* Philadelphia: Trinity, 1990.

———. "History and Development of Mark's Gospel (From Mark to *Secret Mark* and 'Canonical' Mark)." Pages 35–57 in *Colloquy on New Testament Studies: A Time for Reappraisal and Fresh Approaches.* Edited by Bruce Corley. Macon, Ga.: Mercer University Press, 1983.

———. Response to Reginald H. Fuller. Pages 29–32 in *Longer Mark: Forgery, Interpolation, or Old Tradition?* Edited by W. Wuellner. Protocol of the Eighteenth Colloquy; Berkeley: Center for Hermeneutical Studies, 1976.

———. "The Secret Gospel of Mark." Pages 408–11 in *The Complete Gospels.* Edited by Robert J. Miller. Sonoma, Calif.: Polebridge, 1994.

Koppenhaver, Katherine M. *Attorney's Guide to Document Examination.* Westport, Conn.: Quorum, 2002.

Lawrence, Irene. Recorder, "Minutes of the Colloquy of 7 December 1975." Pages 56–71 in *Longer Mark: Forgery, Interpolation, or Old Tradition?* Edited by W. Wuellner. Protocol of the Eighteenth Colloquy; Berkeley: Center for Hermeneutical Studies, 1976.

Lemaire, André. "Burial Box of James the Brother of Jesus." *BAR* 28.6 (2002): 24–33.

Love, Harold. *Attributing Authorship: An Introduction.* Cambridge: Cambridge University Press, 2002.

Marcus, Joel. *Mark 1–8: A New Translation with Introduction and Commentary.* ABD 27. New York: Doubleday, 2000.

Mees, M. *Die Zitate aus dem Neuen Testament bei Clemens von Alexandrien.* QVC 2. Bari: Instituto di Letteratura Cristiana Antica, 1970.

Meier, John P. *A Marginal Jew: Rethinking the Historical Jesus.* ABDL 1. New York, Doubleday, 1991.

Metzger, Bruce M. "Literary Forgeries and Canonical Pseudepigrapha," *JBL* 91 (1972): 3–24.

———. *Reminiscences of an Octogenarian.* Peabody, Mass.: Hendrickson, 1997.

Meyer, Marvin. *Secret Gospels: Essays on Thomas and the Secret Gospel of Mark.* Harrisburg: Trinity, 2003.

Mitchell, Margaret M. "Patristic Counter-Evidence to the Claim that 'The Gospels Were Written for All Christians.'" *NTS* 51 (2005): 36–79.

Mohler, R. Albert, Jr. "Modern Theology: The Disappearance of Hell." Pages 15–42 in *Hell Under Fire: Modern Scholarship Reinvents Eternal Punishment.* Edited by Christopher W. Morgan and Robert A. Peterson. Grand Rapids: Zondervan, 2004.

Munro, Winsome. "Women Disciples: Light from Secret Mark." *JFSR* 8 (2001): 48, n. 5.

Murgia, Charles E. "Secret Mark: Real or Fake?" Pages 35–40 in *Longer Mark: Forgery, Interpolation, or Old Tradition?* Edited by W. Wuellner. Protocol of the Eighteenth Colloquy; Berkeley: Center for Hermeneutical Studies, 1976.

Musurillo, Herbert. "Morton Smith's Secret Gospel." *Thought* 48 (1973): 327–31.

Neusner, Jacob. *Are There Really Tannaitic Parallels to the Gospels? A Refutation of Morton Smith.* SFSHJ 80. Atlanta: Scholars, 1993.

Nickell, Joe. *Detecting Forgery: Forensic Investigation of Documents.* Lexington: University Press of Kentucky, 1996.

————. *Pen, Ink & Evidence: A Study of the Writing and Writing Materials for the Penman, Collector, and Document Detective*. New Castle, Del.: Oak Knoll, 2003.

Nineham, Dennis. Review of *The Secret Gospel*. *JTS* 27 (1976): 195–97.

Orna, Mary Virginia, et al. "Applications of Infrared Microspectroscopy to Art Historical Questions about Medieval Manuscripts." *Archaeological Chemistry* 4 (1988): 270–88.

Osborn, Albert S. *Questioned Documents*. 2d ed. Albany: Boyd Printing, 1929.

Osborn, Eric. "Clement of Alexandria: A Review of Research, 1958–1982." *SecCent* 3 (1983): 225.

Papadopoulos-Kerameus, Athanasios. ῾Ιεροσολυμιτικη Βιβλιοθηκη. 1894. Repr. Brussels: Culture & Civilisation, 1963.

Parker, Pierson. "An Early Christian Cover-up?" *The New York Times*, July 22, 1973.

Petersen, William L. "The Genesis of the Gospels." Pages 33–65 in *New Testament Textual Criticism and Exegesis: Festschrift J. Delobel*. Edited by A. Denaux. BETL 161. Leuven: Leuven University Press, 2002).

Price, Robert M. "Second Thoughts about the Secret Gospel." *BBR* 14 (2004): 127–32.

Pring, J. T., ed. *The Pocket Oxford Greek Dictionary*. Oxford: Oxford University Press, 1995.

Quesnell, Quentin. "The Mar Saba Clementine: A Question of Evidence." *CBQ* 37 (1975): 48–67.

————. "A Reply to Morton Smith." *CBQ* 38 (1976): 200–203.

Rendell, Kenneth W. *Forging History: The Detection of Fake Letters and Documents*. Norman: University of Oklahoma Press, 1994.

Rosenmeyer, Patricia A. *Ancient Epistolary Fictions: The Letter in Greek Literature*. Cambridge: Cambridge University Press, 2001.

Schenke, Hans-Martin. "The Mystery of the Gospel of Mark." *SecCent* 4 (1984): 65–82.

Schleiermacher, F. E. D. *Über den sogenannten ersten Brief des Paulos an den Timotheos*. Berlin: 1807. Repr. Friedrich Schleiermacher's sämtliche Werke 1.2. Berlin: 1836.

Schuler, Mark. *Decoding Mark, Review of Biblical Literature* [http://www.bookreviews.org] (2004).

Sellew, Philip. "Secret Mark and the History of Canonical Mark." Pages 242–57 in *The Future of Early Christianity: Essays in Honor of Helmut Koester*. Edited by Birger A. Pearson. Minneapolis: Fortress, 1991.

Smith, Morton. *Clement of Alexandria and a Secret Gospel of Mark*. Cambridge, Mass.: Harvard University, 1973.

———. "Clement of Alexandria and Secret Mark: The Score at the End of the First Decade." *HTR* 75 (1982): 449–61.

———. "Comments on Taylor's Commentary on Mark." *HTR* 48 (1955): 21–64.

———. "The Description of the Essenes in Josephus and the Philosophumena." *Hebrew Union College Annual* 29 (1958): 273–313.

———. "'Ελληνικὰ χειρόγραφα ἐν τῇ Μονῇ τοῦ ἁγίου Σάββα" ["Greek manuscripts in the monastery of St. Saba"]. Translated by K. Michaelides. Νέα Σιών [*New Zion*] 52 (1960): 251.

———. "The Image of God: Notes on the Hellenization of Judaism, with Especial Reference to Goodenough's Work on Jewish Symbols." *Bulletin of the John Rylands Library* 40 (1958): 473–512.

———. "In Quest of Jesus." *New York Review of Books* 25, no. 20, December 21, 1978.

———. "The Manuscript Tradition of Isidore of Pelusium." *HTR* 47 (1956): 205–10.

———. *Maqbilot ben haBesorot le Sifrut haTanna'im*. Ph.D. Dissertation: Hebrew University, 1948. Revised English translation, *Tannaitic Parallels to the Gospels*. JBL Monograph Series 6. Philadelphia: Society of Biblical Literature, 1951.

———. "Monasteries and their Manuscripts." *Archaeology* 13, no. 3 (1960): 175.

———. "New Fragments of Scholia on Sophocles' *Ajax*." *GRBS* 3 (1960): 40–42.

———. "Notes on Goodspeed's 'Problems of New Testament Translation.'" *JBL* 64 (1945): 501–14.

————. "On the Authenticity of the Mar Saba Letter of Clement."
    CBQ 38 (1976): 196–99.

————. "The Present State of Old Testament Studies." JBL 88
    (1969): 19–35. Reprinted in Studies in the Cult of Yahweh. Vol. 1.
    Pages 37–54. Edited by Shaye J. C. Cohen. RGRW 130. 2 vols.
    Leiden: Brill, 1996.

————. "Regarding Secret Mark: A Response by Morton Smith to
    the Account of Per Beskow." JBL 103 (1984): 624.

————. The Secret Gospel: The Discovery and Interpretation of the
    Secret Gospel According to Mark. New York: Harper & Row, 1973.

————. "Σύμμεικτα: Notes on Collections of Manuscripts in
    Greece." Ἐπετηρὶς Ἑταιρείας Βυζαντιῶν Σπουδῶν [Journal of
    the Society for Byzantine Studies] 26 (1956): 380–93.

————. "An Unpublished Life of St. Isidore of Pelusium." In
    Εὐχαριστήριον. Edited by G. Konidaris. Athens, 1958.

Somers Harold, and Fiona Tweedie. "Authorship Attribution and
    Pastiche." Computers and the Humanities 37 (2003): 407–29.

Speyer, Wolfgang. Die literarische Fälschung im heidnischen und
    christlichen Altertum: eine Versuch ihrer Deutung. Munich: Beck,
    1971.

Stählin, Otto, ed. Clemens Alexandrinus. GCS. Leipzig: Hinrichs,
    1905.

Stroumsa, Guy G. "Comments on Charles Hedrick's Article: A
    Testimony." JECS 11 (2003): 147–53.

Swanson, Reuben J. New Testament Greek Manuscripts: Mark.
    Sheffield: Sheffield Academic Press, 1995.

Taylor, Vincent. The Gospel According to St. Mark: The Greek Text
    with Introduction, Notes, and Indexes. London: Macmillan, 1952.

Theissen, Gerd, and Annette Merz. The Historical Jesus: A Compre-
    hensive Guide. Translated by John Bowden. Minneapolis:
    Fortress, 1998.

Treu, Ursula. "Vorwort zur zweiten Auflage." Clemens Alexandrinus
    4.1. GCS 39.1. Berlin: Akademie-Verlag, 1980.

Vailhé, Siméon. "Les écrivains de Mar-Saba." Échos d'Orient 2
    (1898): 1–11, 33–47.

Voss, Isaac. Epistolae genuinae S. Ignatii Martyris. Amsterdam: J.
    Blaeu, 1646.

Weimar, J. S. *The Piltdown Forgery*. Oxford: Oxford University Press, 1955. 2d ed. 2004.

West, Clive E., et al. "Effect of Iodized Salt on the Colour and Taste of Food." UNICEF No. PD/95/009 (June 1995). http://www.micro nutrient.org/Salt_CD/4.0_useful/4.1_fulltext/pdfs/4.1.4.pdf.

White, John L. *Light from Ancient Letters*. Philadelphia: Fortress, 1986.

Wuellner, W., ed. *Longer Mark: Forgery, Interpolation, or Old Tradition?* Protocol of the Eighteenth Colloquy. Berkeley: Center for Hermeneutical Studies, 1976.

Young, D., ed. *Theognis*. 2d ed. Leipzig: Teubner, 1971.

Index